MW00774463

A

Glimmer

in the

Dark

Samman
Akbarzada

THOUGHTCATALOG.COM

Published by Thought Catalog Books, an imprint of Thought Catalog, a digital magazine owned and operated by The Thought & Expression Company LLC, an independent media organization founded in 2010 and based in the United States of America. For stocking inquiries, contact stockists@shopcatalog.com.

Produced by Chris Lavergne and Noelle Beams
Art direction and design by KJ Parish
Creative editorial direction by Brianna Wiest
Circulation management by Isidoros Karamitopoulos

thoughtcatalog.com | shopcatalog.com

First Edition, Limited Edition Pressing
Printed in the United States of America

ISBN 978-1-949759-54-9

Introduction

What is poetry but a moment of weakness, and what is art if not finding pleasure in one's suffering? There is an eerie beauty in pain; even if we were the ones writing our fate, we would have probably, as well, written fragments of gloom to elevate the thrill.

Like all other art forms, literature is not only for comfort but also for coping with the atrocities of dear life, forcing us to crawl under our skin until it feels right and we can breathe again. Like-minded poets have inspired me to write fearlessly, be myself, run out of sad words, and not feel guilty about it. Music and lyrics inspire me perhaps even more profoundly than literature. This influence has given a sort of elusive style to my words. Poems are not constructed to be lenient in tone with satisfying, expectantly familiar conclusions. Instead, they are formed like waves of classical symphonies at the peak of collapsing while enveloped in optimistic gloom. By ending lethargic days with honest pieces, for ephemeral moments, we are at peace. Its aftereffects can be lasting; lovely it is to drench in a mellowed aura while the world crumbles around us. I aspire *A Glimmer In The Dark* to be that sanctuary.

I think it is life in general, but we get the even more ephemeral version of it. Living life as an Afghan or being from any country tormented by war, the saddest part is that you never get the chance to cherish your people for a satisfactory amount of time. It is a constant race, everything. You are always running, an endless trip. The only stable place you have is the mirage of your home built in the warzone. However, the good thing is that memories now mean the most to you; you will now live and die for them. Pictures and albums will be the most crucial thing you own because that was what you could bring with you from a dead past—one you must mourn in silence. You cannot scream forever in a never-ending funeral, now can you?

Maybe you could not understand the uncertainty of your mother or the overwhelming suggestions of your father, but now you do, very well, and perhaps now you are exactly like them, even though you had said you wouldn't ever be. No sense of home; home is not four walls and a ceiling because you have seen how it collapses in seconds. Home is the people who wretched with us and made it alive by salvaging each other's fragments. It makes us love them more; that is all we can do. War might be evil, but it is only through its ruins that we find a kind of treasure others are unaware of: the value of being together, the certain truth that tomorrow is never promised. May you savor that bittersweet sentiment scattered throughout these pages.

What I love most about poetry is that poems are not made up of mere metaphors. Poetry binds stars, the moon, galaxies, and the universe; it binds flowers, rivers, oceans, and nature to inevitable words. It connects, it unites, and that is breathtakingly beautiful. I have brought my sparkle of connections to *A Glimmer In The Dark* and my mother's too, as the first ten Dari poems are hers. She has been my inspiration from day one; I feel honored to share her beautiful poetry in these pages.

Amidst the isolating chaos that a wanderer must go through, in between endless hours of writing, I find a certain tranquility in it; each piece is my sweet escape from reality. The write-ups created in that phase are daring so enjoy the abandoned questions you will encounter in *A Glimmer In The Dark* and answer each for yourself. Feel weary, halt the ever-spinning, dwell in each poem, and then may the happy poem make you smile afterward. Have a taste of what goes through my mind. It is not always sweet, but it is worth the endeavor.

Maybe a part of us is forever left behind. Maybe there was a happier version of life that we never got to live. Maybe some pains do not have a lesson and are only endured, some scars never fade away, and these high winds will bring us closer. Maybe that is the purpose of storms, and maybe healing is making peace with all of these notions. But, despite all of that, I still think that what matters the most is that we do not let our hearts die at the end of the day.

کردم به هر طرف که نیافتم نشان دوست

رفتم به هر دری که ندادند وفای دوست

شد سالها که بار عمر ما کند بیان

جز مطلب دنیا نکند رخ نگایی دوست

قانون جنگل آمده چو رسم دهر ما

هر کی که داشت قدرت و باشد نمای دوست

مست اند همه به نشه بی خبر ز آخرت

کر دن دغه به دین خود ما را چی کاری دوست

خاموش نمود زمانه مرا لیک بار بار

از لوح این قلم بکنم شرح حال دوست

Souvenir

Laugh at how there are no more
Sad words left to use
Run out of their synonyms as well
Make heartbreaks your excuse
For making restarting a lifestyle
And with your tears, revive the dead
Sing your broken chapters
Among the perfect chorus
Let your ripped sheets stand out
Highlight the promising parts
And when it gets heavy
Leave a comma to pause
But my dear
As long as the pages are ivory
And you have ink running in your veins
Keep bleeding
You're not bleeding in vain

If we knew it was the last picture
Would we still be so happy?
Smiling ear to ear
If we knew one was leaving
Would we stay a little longer?
Holding each other near
If only we knew the blurry faces wouldn't matter
I see them blurred regardless
Despite all the heaviness
Glad the picture doesn't tear

Who gave me the right
To wish for growing
I thought the adult conversations
Were truly funny
Or top secrets I had to know
It's all about bills and money
Their broken laughs sound hollow
I want to hug them all
But I, myself
First, have to calm down
Make the news boring again
Bring back the old Disney
I want to ask lost friends
If they missed me
Monsters under the bed were kinder
Than the pretty angels of today
The bedbugs never bit my toes
But I got damaged anyway
I hope the world was happier
And I wasn't betrayed
I don't want a view like this
Be taken to my grave
Oblivion was a gift
I'm so sick of knowing
Who gave me the right
To wish for growing

Tonight, I set you free
For all that you've suffered
I'm sorry
For the times I shut you down
Then called you wild
Only let you speak when no one was around
And later all that was said, I denied
I felt deep what you wanted
But by a disguised assassin
You were once again daunted
Yes, I've known you very well
It's been all pretend
I'm sorry
I looked you in the eyes and said it to you
Poured it all on the only one I knew
Made you escape when you wanted to stay
And to drown a little more I told you to wait
I'm sorry
These walls weren't built out of love
And the scary, hefty guard feeds out of fear
But I'll give it a hug
Then you run
I've been selfish to the selfless
And I kept you all to myself
You're no longer my hostage
Maybe it'll be better for your health
Tonight, I set you free
But my weary captive, in this tall tower it'll be lonely
Sometimes take heart
Please do come back to me

Honesty
You've brought the truth to my life;
I won't dare to deny you
I can't help but be the most me I've
ever been, only around you
A cocoon learns to fly
You listen to my silence and answer with hues
With all the beautiful colours your aura holds
A glitching light begins to shine
Rest your head on my shoulder and
let's talk about life again
Then be the only ones laughing at the things only we get
In a heartbeat, for you, I would die
It's all about you and I
Me and you
My favourite, I love you
Sediqa ♥

When I'm alone
I have strange wishes
I pray for the door to open on its own
And for you to be on the other side
It opens and it's the wind
For us to see is a major sin
Or maybe you're there and it's true
But there's no use
I can't see you
So I make up a dream
Lucid one and sometimes it feels
As if then is when I'm living
The rest is just not quitting
I imagine you descending from a star
The one that is the farthest of all
So I could look at you longer
Since once you're closer
You fade away
There's no way
In this lifetime
To be together
You're gone
And you're gone forever

What does it take to feel something?
Must it be a storm to enjoy the gloomy clouds?
Bottle up until it rains
Must it be to seep by thorns?
To touch the guarded flowers, around
Bleed and bleed in vain
So much it takes just to feel something

The power's out
There's a creak
And I can already see her feet
Gently she puts the torch
Behind my locked door
And leaves
She knows well I like the dark
But I don't mind her sparks
My soulmate
To whom I've never confessed
Yet she knows me so well
Answered with silence
Questions I've concealed
But she hears
And she sees
My best friend
Seen me in such a mess
But we laughed like best pals
This bond is written in the stars
My mother
Without you
Where would I be?

Life's turning into a museum
Memories at the display
Trying to stay amused
Looking at the ghostly monuments
And they see right through
A living statue
Wishing for one to whisper
It's so quiet
Are any still alive?
I think their lips move
But there's one thing loud
Beating fast again
Slow down for me
They'll find out
This statue has a heart

I wondered...
What's so special about being helpless and in constant need
In need of affirmation and long hugs
In need of longing permissions, given after dramatic cries
In need of sweets and pleased friends
In need of bitter cough syrup at nights
In need of pretty Band-Aids to pay for the fun
In need of screaming 'goodnight' a hundred times
And still, we're yearning to be in need again
It is not knowing
Not knowing was so special
Exotic little bundles of joy
We all were once upon a time

A film is playing before my eyes
In a dreamy filter
Glitching in little, little sparkles
These characters are so beautiful
It takes my breath away
I want it to halt
When they look at each other and laugh
My mother has the sweetest one
I'll live by this pause
Forevermore

Don't ask for a name just to forget
But crave to pursue its meaning
The story of each letter, as it is voiced
Don't say it
But recite it until you sing it like your favourite song
Don't write it down
If you have no space left to engrave it forevermore
Don't ask for names
Don't ask for friendships
If you see it as a name
And just another friend

When I was little
I thought the world was black and white in the past
Yet, now I realise...
That was the time of true colours

Ignore me tonight
Or, if you might, forever
Since I like to be alone with my loneliness together
A lover of the night
A complainer at day
Since the gloom devours shallowness
And in the light
They only talk about the weather
Let me be alone
With my lonesomeness together

Capture this moment with your shimmering eyes
I'll save it inside my heart
Among the albums I cherish the most
We won't need anything else
As long as these memories are caught

If it happened the other way
And I had said goodbye to the girl I
hadn't seen in thirteen years
What would I be thinking about now?
Would she still remember my name?
I wouldn't have to search for hers every day
In every single search bar
Strangers and strangers and strangers as I scroll
But, would she remember my face?
Frizzy hair peeking out from our hairbands
Staining our blue uniforms with fries and ketchup
Circling the playground
Talking about our little lives
What would we say if we met now?
I'm not fun anymore
Does she smile remembering my poem?
Because I still write for her
The perfect sharpened pencil
The right side of the notebook
Was all that mattered
The sound of the bells
Running on the grounds
Screaming at the uncle standing in the canteen
Raising twenty rupees, struggling through the crowd
The only struggle we cared about
The smile of the auntie who teased us with nicknames
Is she alive?
If we had the chance to say goodbye
Perhaps we could say hello again

Let's make the rain our chance to dance
Let's make the sun our reason to shine
Let's make the nights our mystery of wandering together
Let's make the love our longing to hold hands
Let's make life our promise to be a forever
Let's make excuses to be happy

Will the colour red remind you of her?
Or will it make you hate the colour altogether
Does the moon smile at you at night?
Or do you hate the idea she looks
at it too, in her chilly weather
Will all that you love detach from her name?
Or all that you love will be hated forever

What do you bleed my dear?
'Cause it's not blood
And yet you're hurt
It's not tears
I'm never the one who wiped one
Is it fear?
Holding you back
How long till I get a chance?
Show me what I can't see
Tell me, what do you bleed?

Where do we go when there's no land to hold the weight?
No space for you
Nowhere feels right
What to see when the only time you're at
peace is when you close your eyes?
Every gaze tells a sad story
Everywhere strangers passing by
The blackness feels familiar
A kind of sadness that can be borne
Better than all the colours we've seen
Why say anything when nothing will change?
No letters able to convey
Scrambled twigs, thoughts
No ears to like honesty
Can't reach their hearts
Where to go when nowhere feels like home?

That stubborn smile
Fears away the audacity of life
To never assume it'll be lived in agony
Rips off scary reasons
Rooting in your anxious mind
May it live a hundred years, my dear
That stubborn smile :)

When I was little
The moon was following me
From the window of the car I stared at it
As it was smiling at me
I looked at the moon
When the dark was gallowing me
I was flying around back then
I was near the clouds back then
I was safe and sound back then
I was glad and proud back then
When I was little
I spoke with the girl, her reflection on the mirror
She was happy, she was silly, she was a winner
She had her own world to live in
She had important missions to win
She was strong, she was bold, she wasn't a sinner
She was bound back then
She was fun to be around back then
She was safe and sound back then

To know how lonely you are
With what you call together
How will it feel?
They're nothing more than that stranger
Crossing the street
To know how wasted you are
With what you call memories
How will it be?
A lifetime of nothing more than heavy lumps
Salt in the sea
You're trying to make it sweet

So out of place
So out of order
A raven jigsaw
Trying to fit
In what was already fixed
Hued frame stayed the same
Too pretty to be changed
Too formal to be stared at
So it stopped the chase
And bloomed out of borders
Once a piece
Now the piece
On its own
The raven jigsaw

I'm still locked up in a ballad
Dancing with the tied curtain
Singing Disney songs
Talking with an imaginary friend
About saving the cosmos all day long
Now, someone's singing for survival
And for the apocalypse so it would stop
I'm still locked up in those wistful nights
Sleeping wrapped in a doll's arms
On her hat was written Candy
Always called her Sandy
Thought that was her name all along
Now, it's hard to differentiate the inanimate
I'm still locked up in a million games
Resident Evil 4 was chilling
While playing, its intro music
Made me feel some type of way
Swivelling to get dizzy
And laughing at the spinning world
I miss that little girl
Now, we are the living dead with no escape
I'm still locked up in that mirror
When I didn't know what beautiful meant
Or that ugly was a thing
All I could see were my beautiful friends
Now, their faces are fading
Forgetting names and memories are running low
I'm still locked up in a yesterday
But tomorrow isn't letting me go

Whist
Hush my dear
It's so much better
Mist
Yes, those tears
Secretly scattered
Abyss
To live in fear
Yet, nothing matters
Anymore...

You can't be just a passenger
In your own home
Sing with the flock
Your sweetest songs
Burn down, free fall with them
Amidst chaos and mayhem
Exchange one of your torn limbs
And stitch your wings
Make them your part
And hurt for them too
They are your people
Love them while you can still do

What if I told you that is healing
When there are no more band-aids
Left for you to hide
Ugly scars and bleeding wounds
And it drips off your soul
Droplets grow cold
Red pearls on the floor
Collect and combine
Wear them with pride
What if I told you that is healing
When there are no routes left to land
For your numb feet and broken hands
Look around and gather
Each of your torn feathers
For a change and a rest
Fancy a new downy nest
What if I told you that is healing
When the arch holding a smile tears
No more ego, nor bloody fear
Can halt the aching flood
That's been long forecasting to come
In between violent screaming
What if I told you
You are healing

سال‌ها را هجرت تو ای وطن دردم بداد

لطف آن سرو خروشان آب تو زجرم بداد

آمدم گیرم تورا آغوش وطن ای حرمتم

مردمان سفله گو دامان پاکت ای وطن شرمم بداد

غیرت تاریخ تو اندر جهان مانند لعل

حیف و صد حیفت کشم در دست نامردان شدی شرمم بداد

حیله و فسق و فساد نشه ها سر گرمیت

ای کجاست آن غیرت مردان دیرینت وطن سردم بداد

من خاموش دارم دعا ای هم وطن آمین بگو

پاک خواهم دامن پاکت وطن از هر بلا خیرم بداد

Motherland

Damn the war
I'll be running in the warzone
Seeing it as the playground
We circled in ecstasy
Hurl your bloody bombs
I'll flow with their gusts
Drift to the misty sky
And sing with the songbirds
Watch me prom over mines
Outlined with my blood
Throwing pellets
Playing hopscotch
With the ghost of my best friend
To hell with your guns
I'll feel the bullet
As a tossed rose
From my devoted lover
I'll turn around
Falling on a soft spot
Smiling with my eyes closed
Reconciled

I'm a child, with big dreams
And bigger responsibilities
For once I would like to taste
Those colourful cookies on display
An eyesore across the street
I smile to frowning faces while selling sweets
Father didn't make it
And my mother is slowly fading
Cute little siblings I have
But ample food is what we lack
I have plenty of stories to tell
Scarier than the hell
That you're afraid of
For that fear is when I get
A penny, torn slippers, dried bread
You ask me to pray for you
While you leave forsaking me in abyss
I wonder if there's a place for me in there too
Or God doesn't like dirty faces and fetid shoes
My eyes flicker when it flashes
Cameras avert and hopeful lies I'm handed
Take me to the unknown wilderness
Creatures there might not be this merciless
This place is too wild
For a working child

We start with ballads
Then words arrive
Changing them to laments
With broken hearts, it rhymes

In each of the empty chambers
Feeble voices echo
A child's laughter
Levitating and off he goes

A lullaby for the sleepless daughter
The restless father sings
Bullets tick with the time
She throbs in his damaged limbs

A woman is chanting a name
Facing merry pictures on the wall
They break the knot to tie his chin
And tell her to be silent for he is gone

In a mother's dream
Her son is alive
Life for her is a deadly drifter
She's just waiting for to pass by

I had started with a ballad
Then these words arrived
Changing it to a lament
With a broken heart, it rhymes

I miss the way wind blew in my motherland
Lifting its soil, heaving my heart
In form of midnight murmurs or dancing curtains
It would pass by as I was merged in the dark
Kabul was lightless sometimes
But somehow our spirits were not
I miss the sight of Luna I was used
to looking at, in my motherland
She had a smile there, and I wasn't a wayfarer
Searching an endless gloaming
Trying to find her somewhere
I miss hearing people speak in the
tongue of my motherland
Getting used to skipping heartbeats
When another dispersed speaks
Among the saddest eyes, they'll ever be
Kabul was bleeding always
But I had hoped to paint it green
I miss saying the name of my motherland
Without getting teary-eyed
Wondering how many farewells
I said disguised as a goodbye
Forsaking myself and all of it behind
Afghanistan was a hopeful ray
But its sun will return
One day...

The purple clouds popped
Ebony mists birthed from them
It streams black tears
Falling from a cursed sky
Over the people who had hoped
Nature would be kinder
But bleeding oceans
Can only evaporate
To make you bleed further
I don't think like a poet anymore
Raindrops aren't pearls
Nor gentle kisses which caress
In my motherland
It pours over young graves
Or on working children sleeping
Wrecking their only sweet escape
Popping their purple clouds

Today I passed by a land
The land of the dead Emperor they call it
I saw a baby with a bullet stuck in her leg
She was born and her mother was dead
Not by child birthing
But by something that I refuse to call men
The nurses were the first ones to get shot
I was the wind that closed the door
After they left the room in holes
I passed by a land
The saddest country they call it
I saw a dreamer, sleeping
His head over the floor
As he was bleeding
He studied law
In the most unlawful soil
And they killed him
I was the wind that informed his mother
In the same class
I saw a girl
Hanging from the shattered window
She couldn't escape
Her dire fate
She was born in the place
Where lives are meant to be survived
Just so they could die
I was the wind passing by

We were born with wings
That could only fly to prisons
Spent lives dodging barbed wires
Bruised like fallen angels
They say we're free now
Have my torn wings

We were handed keys
That open the gates of hell
But they want us to go to heaven
Exiled from homes we dwell
They say we're free now
Have my good deeds

We were told to speak up
With stitched lips
Words voiced merged with blood
But still, nobody listened
They say we're free now
Have my frantic poems

I wish it was a lie
But freedom used to mean a thing
Once upon a time
They say we're free now
Have my freedom

Girls on the line
Ready to be sold
The shape of her teary eyes
Adds up to the number
Her arching brows
Could be her escape
To slide and fly away
But it's another detail
Adds up to the number
Each strand of her hair
Tells a sweet tale
But her stitched lips
And their deaf ears
Adds up to the number
Her pale skin
Is compared to moonlight
Untouched and fragile
Adds up to the number
My sisters on the line
Ready to be sold

Words don't come to me
I had feared this day
And I'm pretending to write a poem
Since it's been ten days
Silence allied with chaos
Peace, a lost friend
Built homes on battlefields
War is the landlord held
We pay every twenty years
Our lifeless souls are in debt
Songbirds flew away
The winds crushed them down
Skies do not want us
Nor does the merciless ground
A million broken dream
Carved into a nightmare
To hide away from existence
There must be somewhere
Even hope has its limits
For eternities it's just us
And the endless abyss
While waiting for a new start
We forgot
This must be the end

Death was lurking in home
Hearts didn't beat for fear
We must've got out
It started beating
But half-heartedly
Death isn't near
But life is forlorn
Four walls and a ceiling
But it doesn't feel like home
The fire cackles
We don't feel warm
Safe in foreign lands
With our broken hands
And frigid bones

Maybe in another dimension
It's snowing right now
Working children
Build snowman there
Soldiers march to fields
And snow fight
Maybe in another dimension
It rains flowers
And blooms raindrops
There is a moon
But not her scars
The sun is frozen
But our hearts are not
Maybe in another dimension
Lovers can't love
But they want to
Folks don't hate
But they can
Poets don't exist
Every word is poetry
Maybe in another dimension
Tears cry out for themselves
But rivers are silent
A foreign tongue spoken
But hearts understand
In a strange world with strangers
But maybe I'd know who I am

If tomorrow the war killed her
And freed her soul
May you live your life in peace
And may you breathe forevermore
If the bullet went through her heart
Know it would never touch
Where she holds you close
She'll hold you dear forevermore
If she's thrown, if she's blown
Watch her fall in your arms softly
And stay there forevermore
If she bled, don't you shed a tear no more
Paint two connected hearts
They will beat forevermore
If tonight the war killed her
And freed her soul
She'll meet you in your dreams
Forever and evermore

Let's dive into the black void
Of our broken flag
And stay there
We'll draw stars
And paint a moon
A whole other universe
They won't find us
Let's evade these red rivers
The blood of our loved ones
Is all converged together
You and I
With our deprived hearts
On this shipwreck
We're still afloat
Let's find the green blooms
It's been lost forever
We've been sowing tombs
And reaping sorrow
To those who are gone
Is there more to this world
Than death and war?
Let's run to mountains
And never be seen
Stay close to me
Have my last breaths
And wave one more time
Oh my beloved
Black, Red, and Green

I was running out of ways to describe blood
But now you showed me bleeding children
Collapsed on your streets, inhaling dust
If breathing still
For a second I forgot who I was
I was running out of ways to define hypocrites
But for you, they fight for peace
Just to leave you in pieces
Never have the world loved silence
Yet they watch you wither in violence
With their filthy mouths shut
I was running out of ways to write for your women
But now they pierce her with bullets
Or fancy a slave for their lust
Whether submit to the embodiment of disgust
Or she's a thing left undone
I was running out of ways to illustrate pain
But now you've made me numb
There's nothing left to grieve for
I'm no longer hurt
Dear one
I can't thank you enough

How am I doing? How are any of us doing? You dared to ask, I must dare to answer. The question brings up leaden lumps to our throats, for we are trying to be numb. When asked, we suddenly can feel how we are, but we choke on words and can't tell. An endless loophole of uncomfortable feelings.

I may write, but after fighting for a will, bleeding the same words gets dire, and not doing is strangling. So here I go again.

He may sing, but the saddest verses of loss and a broken heart. His silence sounds the grimmest. She may laugh, but dear God, it's so hollow. You'd rather hear her midnight cries.

The past had never been so romanticized in our unsettled heads and the future had never been so dead. The present, I'd rather not. Days are turning to nights, nights are turning to days, we're aging, and bestowing youth for a lost cause.

Mothers are baking with the love that remains in them, but we still savour poison. Fathers are patting our backs and coming up with their jokes, but we still catch them staring into the abyss. Who dares to gaze into those children's gleaming eyes then say, we failed you? Girls are already adjusting to the life that's playing before their eyes, like a horror film that never seems to end. A life without life itself.

How are we doing, you asked?

Find the song
That will answer
For their deaf ears & our caged lips
The question I've failed to ask
The answer you've failed to give
They won't say
We were silent
Play it loud
So they stop asking
The birds stop chirping
The sun stops singing
Clouds will prom
And merge with lethargic drops
They won't know
It's covering me and you
Voice the letters
The saddest poem
With its disorganised rhymes
Let it sync with a heart
That beats the same way
They won't hear
Broken things
Paint the frame
Draw us happy
So we don't die
Not knowing how we smiled
They won't find us
In another dimension
In another life

A ghost lingering in a warzone
Dies many times
Forgot when was the first time
When it lost it
And it has been lost since
Cannot end
Cannot start
Only walks
In rounds
Just to see
They've never stopped
More dead flowers
Plucked from the ground
Sometimes it's bullets
Sometimes it's words
Passes through
Forgot when was the first time
When it hurt it
And it has been numb since
Cannot feel
Cannot heal
Only sees
A distant war
And it goes on
Again

Not an outsider
How can one be when there's no way out?
Not an insider
How can one be when all you feel is indifference?
A passenger in one's own homeland
That's what it is

If I'm your next target
Let me paint red circles around me
From the blood of those you feared
All those killed by your coward self
I want them to make me stand out
Would you dare to come close?
If I'm your next target
Let me kiss the hands of the mother
Sitting in the corners
Fading away softly
You killed her son
Wasn't he too young?
If I'm your next target
Let me carry the message
Of the madman
Smiling with flooded eyes
Can't live, he only suffers
You killed his lover
Does your heart beat?
If I'm your next target
Let me say farewell
To what made
A heartbroken poet
Farewell
To the land
Where our homes lay
You've brought it to its deathbed
How was it before you were born?

I envy their wings
They were singing
Lively leaves were merged with dew
In a blink of an eye
The sky was no longer blue
Swings were swaying but hollow
They ran away
Let them catch a breath
They're the lucky ones who can still do
Be wise enough to know
But to calm down you have to act like fools
Chant the lies to yourself
To that panting Mother don't you dare tell the truth
Strange how I can hear her cries
Is she calling a name?
I can hear that too
I think he had just graduated
She was on her way to school
One by one, eventually it's all of us
But at least, the birds flew...

We're a different breed
We listen to what we must get used to nine months
Never really knew what is fun
We are born and under operation
A bullet pulled out, tomorrow another round
We are children asking for bread
Not candies, an empty can would come in handy
We are students, our blood speared on papers
A fan of education with so many haters
We are delicate youths, levitating and happy
Under bridges, stabbing you to cope with hidden stitches
We're so special, thus
I hope you never become one of us

Dear one
Amidst your catastrophe
There's a child sound asleep
Collapsed on your bleeding street
He's having a sweet dream
Dear one
Amidst your dying days
I see streaming rays
Sinking in gleaming waves
One forgets you're ablaze
Dear one
Amidst your silence
Hypocrites are hiding
Burning you in violence
Fighting for peace

But I had tried
To not be like them
I said I'll be different
We're not our Mothers and Fathers
A new story with exciting plots
Happily ever afters
But I had hoped
I won't face what they had
And use her destiny only in my fictions
You gave me your all, but...
When did your life become mine, mother?
But I had promised
To write my fate and make it rhyme
That is sweet to read
A few commas here and there
Then continue a pleasing ballad
That'll be applauding
Then why now the pen isn't moving?
Too scared to peak
How many pages must be left
And I'm thinking of full stops

If you want to break your heart
Amble on the streets of Kabul
Listen to that stray dog
But ignore the barks you'll hear from some
Cry for the youth, and see what they have become
No dreams, we're too busy burying the past
Everyone is an adult, that four-year-
old has practised how to beg
Stay quiet, don't talk since whatever you'll
listen to will be a disappointment
We murder teenagers for a cell phone
And we live till we're lucky enough to remain alive
Like that fruitless tree, our heads are raised high
I wonder...why?
The stories from an era that I hear, that's where I'm from
Not this
Hopelessly lost
What do I write?
Where do I go?
What do I do?

Now that you're here
The missiles can cross over her
And she'll stand in awe
She won't feel pain
Amidst a meteor shower
Of piercing bullets
Hitting the ground like rain
Now that you're here
She won't run away to live
But run towards death
Where you're standing
With your arms open
Then together you'll fall
Into the abyss
And give it a kiss
Now that you're here
Death feels your only chance
Life never let you meet
It will be your reconciliation
This all was an ephemeral dream
Now that you're here
She can't wait for the apocalypse
Of your little world

I'm afraid
There won't be water pouring down the sink
It'll be cold blood, thicker than my bleeding ink
Sky will pour and it will be red
The sun soaked up all our dead
Their weary souls evaporated
But sadly, we somehow made it
I'm afraid
There won't be any hope to live by
No need to search for reasons to cry
Our tears are ruddy, soaking pillows are wet
Our land on its deathbed
I'm afraid
 I have the same stories my mother had to tell
This tale is reaping scarier, history repeating itself
Our motherland, on its deathbed

An illusion I want to get caught in
Farewell while smiling at the sun
Inside a soft bubble, wandering around bullets and blood
Rose-tinted glasses to see collapsed walls in colours
For a second let me not see, seen enough
In your pretty lies, let me believe, existence is tough
Let's celebrate death, life's been a
never-ending funeral, my love
For you and I, things have never been kind
Now let's watch our homes fall apart softly
A landscape worth a cry
I'm tired

And I see you so close
Lingering around the corner
But when I think of you though
You take a step back
Taking someone else
One flower from each garden and
You're not picky
But it's the blooming ones
That are missing
Fading behind white dresses
They look so pretty
Faces surrounding them restless
Dear death,
We haven't got the chance
To live yet

You're rusting before my eyes
Trying to hold on to you
The stronger you're held
The quicker your grains
Fade away
From my helpless hands
Merging with the wind
Off you go
Leaving traces in the air
Of my childhood
I breathe to recall
To save memories
In the necropolis of a heart
A deceased self
You don't want to be saved
I don't even try
Letting your weary self
Forsake without wishing well
Farewell
You're rusting before my eyes
And I'm letting it

The hands we've kissed
Wonder if the damp earth will keep them warm
Do they tremble, hoping to be held?
I'll clasp them, every shaking hand, in every single dream
Lying hushed beside them, in our graveyard of memories
The last scene captured before our eyes
Saved in our hearts
Wonder if there is any more space left
For cemeteries with pretty pictures
Is this one it?
I'll keep taking them, every single smile of every fading face
In every single dream
Forgetting the facts, making new rememberings
Reminiscing about the last gaze
The last day
The last laugh
The last goodbye
And you know?
I can't help but think of endings
Before saying my hellos

Could someone please tell the world
It is over now and they can open their eyes
Fathers quit and kids are sold
Even the ones reporters called too pretty to be on hold

Schools don't ring bells for my kind
Childish dreams are bound
To the last names of eighty-year-old men
Even girls who are about to turn seven

Lives are at a loss of glee
Souls are deprived of peace
Shops are empty of bread
Even the one next to our once-upon-a-residence

Everything and everyone exceedingly hates us
Malnutrition has become contagious
It is stopping little weary hearts from beating
Even newborns were too exhausted to keep on leading

Please tell them that they don't have
to look away to not see us
We are too busy attending continuous burials
We are preoccupied with what could have been
If our motherland had a chance to live

I'm not at home anymore, but now in a very strange state. I see the uncle selling fresh vegetables from delusional windows. I hear the little girls saying hi to me on their way to the school that is shut down. I feel my best friend's hug, but I don't even know if she's alive. I can see myself here, but where am I?

I'm the living country covered with a shroud that is now my flag. I'm the widowed mothers, starving children, and desperate dads. I'm a million girls fading in the corners of murky rooms. I'm the soldier left with broken badges and unhealed wounds. I know who I am, but who am I?

I'm screams heard by heartless men. An irrelevant tragedy for feminist women. I'm the only kind of myself lost to calamity. A witness at the death of dear humanity.

I know I'm a human, but what am I?

Sometimes
There aren't even city lights
We wear the gloom
And wrap the chill around us till another dawn
The lull city comes to be dead, but we're alive
Curled up in homes, amidst the chaos
We're safe and sound
It's a sad movie and we are the leading stars
I see a sadness in those waiting eyes
And I get hope through their stubborn smiles
Innocently dwelling thug life
But still, even for the whole wide world
I'm not giving my Kabul nights

You load your guns
We'll turn the pages
You pull the triggers
We'll press our pens
Rip us one by one
Beware, there's a hoard of us

Stain us with blood
We'll paint crimson roses
On our ivory scarf
We're retained in hearts
You're just a nightmare
We're a million dream
Many resuming as we sleep

We're legendary stories and can't die
You can't kill us
Look around
We're still alive

To that day
When seeing your best friend
Won't be a miracle
When conversation won't start as
"Did it pass safely?"
When morning tea that would have been drunk
Won't go cold and miserable
When tables won't be hollow, sad
No one dares to sit on that chair lately
When the news host won't be depressed
Won't be historical
When good news would make a
difference, and
I won't run away to save me
Surrendering to hymns, papers, ink
and rhymes to pass the day
When there would be a way, but not the need to escape
Endeavouring, rooting, here it goes
To that day

One day
Flowers will bloom in motherland
May we be the dandelion seeds
Wished upon and set free
Birds will sing in motherland
May we be the gentle breeze
That caress their broken wings
Children will play in motherland
May we be waves of their laughs
Fluttering the tricolour risen flag
Happy tears shall hail
Motherland will prevail
Hearts shall be put in ease
I solemnly believe
Even if you and I
Were forgotten memories
And peculiar essence only to see
It's alright because
Motherland will be free

صبح که من از جا بجستم جلوهء هوشدار کرد

رمز دنیا را چنان دیدم که ما را یک نفس بیدار کرد

ای دریغا سالها دیدم نکردم رطبت این ماجرا

چون همه این مرغکان را از برای لانهء در کار کرد

صبح که هر یک میروند سویی ز سویی پر زنان

از برای آب، دانه زجر ها بر بار کرد

ای که هستیم اشرف المخلوق در دنیای خود

یک پرنده در خجل از خواب غفلت همچنین بیدار کرد

من خاموش محو چنان تقدیر طبیت گشتم

قدرت پروردگار در بی زبان اسرار کرد

Exceptional
Escapist

Depending on words
I'm afraid they're piling
A word is all it takes
For it all to collapse
Running away and away
In an aisle of sad stories
Lurking behind songs
Murmuring morose
Hoping no one heard it
Running away and away
May no hands reach
The caged heart in preach
Camouflaging to rust
A touch is all it takes
For it all to turn to dust
Running away and away

Make this a nightmare
And make me wake up
I won't ever dare
To sleep again
Make me the monster
And hand me the sword
I won't hesitate
To end it all
Make me a way
I'm running out of them
I won't care
To stop
Make this a nightmare
We're clasped in the dark

If I left
What will stay?
Would it be soaking pillows?
Inkless pens
Scrunched papers
In funny ways
They'll laugh at me
Like they always do
So will the walls
And I will muse
A happy room
But a sad aura
Only I can feel
Maybe I'm the reason
Nothing feels real
If I left
What will stay?

A letter to the girl still left in the corners of her
safe haven, I know that to escape, you had to be
left behind. A forlorn part that could never let go,
so she stayed, then she left at the same time.
Who are you, which one are you, where are you?

The one beside the draped but open win-
dows, tasting midnight breeze,
hearing midnight murmurs, merged
with befriended ebony?
Or the weary wanderer, who just can't stop running away?

The pessimistic giving hope, hopelessly, writing
how heavens scent, how damaged wings mend,
how broken hearts amend, behind the bars of hell?
Or the one now in paradise who has mis-
taken the Godforsaken ablaze
for her castaway home?

The hostage smearing her cage, rhyming her com-
plaints, to the ones too far away to listen,
spent and tired, yet singing her cries?
Or the estranged songbird, camouflag-
ing farewells with goodbyes,
flying in foreign skies?

The ghostly presence of the past, or
the uncertain routes ahead,
what are you?

Dear one,
Write back to me, I'm lost

Who even knows what we're afraid of...?
Shouldn't it be these scenarios?
The worst-case ones
Closer than the last breath
Freed from your dusty lips
As it left
Shouldn't it be these visions?
The fortune teller
Who ravages your now
To harmonise it with your future
And your past too
What you're afraid of, is already in you

What are you running from tonight?
Is it letters forming to monsters
Singing in chorus
Unseen seconds
Glimpsed as disasters for us
The hope to live by
Already broken
What are you running from?
Tonight

I can't do you any good
So at least let me not do you any
Sweetheart, don't fall
For a broken thing
It'll merely break you apart

Thousand years have I missed?
Or a thousand lives have I lived?
I miss a past that I never had
A future I envision, that I prefer to never have
Is it the soul that's old?
Or is it this world that's so young?
Youthful and fun
Something I fail to be
Wild waves surrounding an estranged dove
Searching for calmness in chaos, always fails to see
Without even having it
Feels like I've had enough

You can't see it
But it's right behind you
Predicts your every move
Disguised as your shadow
But shadows leave you when it's dark
And that is when this hits you hard
Something inside, monotonous tone
A universe around leaves you so alone
Desperate for a pass out of this mind
Rather be locked somewhere kind
An exceptional escapist
It's obnoxious when it's whist
Dusk and then dew
Running, running, running
And running anew...

If you see her wandering
Tell her to come back home
Tell her those wildernesses are imaginary and
that peace can't be the same as insanity
Tell her that she should know what she's facing and
that there is no red line and she should stop racing
Tell her that nights can't be rendered or
cut if nightmares are awaiting for her
Tell her that days are expecting her life-
less breaths and she must wake up
Tell her that fictions are synonyms with lie
and the sweetest characters are first to die
Tell her that wishes can't be made upon broken
things and her beloved moon is constantly burning
Tell her that their understanding has its limits,
and not be alienated for comfortable sadness
Tell her it's called Earth and not paradise and
a touch of hell is scattered on dear lives
Tell her that writers are known for being
crazy, poets for being a lot more hazy
Don't be weird or they'll know
There's no way for her to go
Tell her to come back
Even if she's lost at home

Disappearing
Merged into thin air around
In midst of strong walls, covered in shrouds
Somewhere high above the thickest clouds
Underneath surface less grounds
Wherever nowhere to be found

I want to run away from the places I take myself
But even if I try, it's an eternal marathon
Each lap, a new invention
Giving it all, struggling for redemption
Are they my creation?
My footsteps, my ademption
The red thread doesn't appear
A deserted race
A failed victory
What if I stopped?

Did the freedom set you free
Or are you now a captive
Hiding from the key
You wrecked chains
Stitched them to your nerves
Look at yourself
A laughing marionette
Dancing to its death
If now you know all the words
Why are your parched lips
Giving seals a silent kiss
Clambered mounts
Just to fall behind
Ancient walls
How can you crush
What's built by tears and blood
Evaded labyrinths
Just to get directions
From your whispering demons
But did the freedom set you free
There is no escape

How deprived of sentience it has all become. For the sake of it to end, one cuts open, holding out a heart, bleeding in shaking hands. Cold droplets form on the snow, inking and camouflaging roses in hopes for a kind word, in hopes they'd understand the disorganised rhythm it cries out. Endeavouring to make something beautiful out of its perishing momentum, none could guess how.

Sadly the thorns never go unnoticed, grown from it, tearing it open, bit by bit. The hurt sometimes makes it run and weep, a sign of bitter roots for people who always dig deep. And it hopelessly got pricked one by one, being pulled back on the run, from vain and its bloody pain, forever failing to find an escape.

Don't pity the vacant heart, it's not there for the plea, just trying its best to let you know what it feels. And even though every wanderer walks over, yet their footprints carry on trails of what they tore and turned away from. They're leading crimson tracks and one follows, carrying a dripping heart, drawing spirited roses.

There must be a shore
For drowning people
I shall build the arch
After saving myself
There must be a grip
For every hand
Drifting in silence
In serene touch wishing to land
One by one I shall pick
After fixing my broken limbs
There must be a place
For us to go
I shall build the arch
Cast away from woe

A fluke you push under the piles
Skimmed like the sad part of a dusted book
You don't want to read it
Now it's lurking inside your chest's nook
But will you really not see it
When that will be all you see
And will you not hear
The narration of your heart
Breathlessly running away
From what your feet are chasing
Turning away your prudent sight
Yet it's the only truth you're facing
But will you really not reach
Where your soul is waiting
And will you not greet
The familiar stranger
Hindering the race
Murmuring your name

ای وطن زادگاه پیرانم تویی

هر چه در وصفت بگویم ای که در جانم تویی

وصف کوه هایت کنم یا چشمه های ناز تو

خلقت آن لایزال هستی که شکرانم تویی

این همه اسرار نعمت های تو

شکر خواهد ای که بی همتای دورانم تویی

هستی و نام و نشانم از تو است پیدا مرا

سر بلند خاموش ترا خواهد که پندارم تویی

A
Glimmer
in the
Dark

How does it feel to know
I'm just as hopeless as you are...?

Bleeding over a lengthy sentence
Commas pause for tears to drop
A full stop that never really ends
Her agony, nor her wordy heart
Writing paragraphs, she sobs
And the night ends forlornly
She continues by leaving it
With three tiny dots...

If I were your heart,
what would you say to me?

Keep it quiet
The world is loud enough
Obnoxiously wild
We don't need good words anymore
It'll just become another noise
Disappearing in the void
Be silent and make it contagious
Silent the world
It's tired

How bad do you have to want it,
so the want would let you have it?

Who were you before?

My dear
In times like these, savour my tears
They'll be plenty for years and years
For a lifetime I'll bestow them to you
My dear
Bear my words
And make sense out of my silence
It's spoken well in my wordy world
My dear
There's nothing much into me
Than a graveyard of memories where tears rain
And sometimes flowers bloom out of nowhere
Rooted by sorrows, they nourish out of covert drops
Provided secretly at the dark
The doves sing for them too, and then together, we muse
Happy flowers over necropolis in fay
Night shall come cloaked in itself
And for a thousand nights, a night will stay
My dear
I'm the nightmare in your sweet dreams
There's nothing more into me

Where do they go?
Thoughtful words
Perfected for moments
That never passed by
My troubled mind
Quiet down for me
Where do they go?
Unexpected dreams
Of perfect moments
Proving wrong
Every single reality
My fading recall
Tonight, be there for me
Where do they go?
Seconds gazed
Perfectly estranged
Befriending a wall
Sheer evenfall
My senses
Come back to me
Where do they go?
Forgotten prays
Sincere perfection
Perhaps a little late
My God

Give my tears back to me

Perhaps by assuming you don't deserve it,
you're only leaving it for someone worse than you...

Will I escape these crumbling walls?
Or for an eternity we will crumble
As I and a guarded heart loathe each one till we rupture
Will I forget these haunting thoughts?
Or for a thousand night long we will mumble
As I and covert voices, project sneak peeks of a dreaded end
Bear the past as we fumble
Will I ever learn to reside?
Or through weary words, forever I will grumble

How many worlds are you living?

Do you shiver?
When her name aches in your nerves
Grows in your bones
Runs through your blood
Explodes in your heart
You still refuse to call it love
Do you hurt?
When nothing matters
No one else
Makes you feel the same
What do you do?
When you feel the truth
And yet you refuse
But deep down, you don't want to
Tell me, do you shiver?

If it's not destined to happen then
why does it happen in the first place?

Isn't it beautiful?
People making a home
Past all their tragedies
Through the tsunami
Holding on to stubborn gravity
Trying to be a soft pillow
And have each other's back
Laugh at his unfunny jokes
Together, they'll be sad
Wars more dramatic than theatres
Loves her enough
His thoughts can't escape her
Figuring out how to respond
To frightened silence
With calm hues of Violet
They paint their damaged walls
Two reconciled souls
Mending hearts

If there was no need for an explanation,
what would you do right now?

And even if we knew all the answers,
we'd fabricate another question, just to not know...

I surrender you to the mountains
I've never put a step on, I won't dare
I surrender you to the luminous skies
I never look for, I'm a stargazer at night-time
I surrender you to the lofty perches, heights terrorise me
I'll never go near
I surrender you since you were never mine

If they asked you why,
Would you even know what to say?

Have you seen your palms?
Or you're blinded by the way
The way they gleam under the sun
Have you seen your eyes!
The way they reflect mine
Have you heard your words?
Or you're too scared to even try
They have the authority to change my world
And I can't even ask them why
Have you seen your lips
The way they curve timidly
Oh dear
I'm afraid you'll be the death of me

ای عمر از دست رفته ام کاری بکن باز آه باز

ای کاروان دشت و دهر راهی بگیر باز آه باز

کردم هزاران شکوه ای خدا بشنو یکی

این مرغ دل دارد دعا دستم بگیر باز آه باز

رحمت ببخش بر حال ما یا خالق روز جزا

آن یاری بی همتا را دارم صدا باز آه باز

یا در کفن کن جان من یا جان ببخش اندر تنم

هستم گناه کار یا غفار اشکی ندام باز آه باز

از سوز دل دارم دعا هر مسجد و منبر ترا

دارد صدا خاموش ترا ای بی خبر باز آه باز

She wanted to be perceived as strong,
it was her biggest weakness...

She is mist
There, but not there
As you grip
She slips away
Covert nothingness in your hands
She will evaporate
Wait for her to form
Then fall in your arms
She is mist
There, but not there
She's everywhere
Anywhere
But, where?
She is mist
Dancing in whist
By yearning eyes
She is kissed
By longing hearts
She is missed
She is mist

How to love her?
When it's foreign to the amateur
Mastered indifference
Now she thinks of her as a know it all
How to hug her?
When she loathes my touch
And when I hate her
She can't get enough
How to make her listen?
When she shut her heart
I don't blame her
But wonder if she talks to God
How to hold her hand?
When she doesn't stop
Make her stay
She's out of my hands

Her ambition you praise today
Will be the reason you leave tomorrow
And you'll get sick of her
Her fragile heart you proudly own today
Will be your bitter regret tomorrow
And you'll get sick of her
Her emotions you keenly understand today
Will be the ocean she'll drown in tomorrow
And you'll get sick of her
Her clinging out of devotion today
Will be the foreign space she'll get lost in tomorrow
And you'll get sick of her
Her hard to know secrets today
Will be your words used against her tomorrow
And you'll get sick of her
Her uniqueness for what you picked her today
Will be the first drying flower tomorrow
And you'll get sick of her

She asked the winds for the answer
And their silence left her speechless
She asked the trees for what's beneath
And their dry spell left her breathless
She asked the rivers to take her with them
And their absence left her worthless
Whatever she touched, died
Yet she was there alive
Despite it all...

       There's a sigh that makes her sound so miserable
       But there are words she lets go through it
       Words that'll make her honest
       But they're irresistible
       So bear her sighs and be glad for her silence
       Let words evade through a sigh
       Don't make them invincible

She was a broken star
Someone needed to make a wish
She was a deserted well
Someone cried replenishing
She was a weakening purpose
Pursued to be remembered
She was a magnet
Stimulated by amorphous shells

                    It hid her well

Naive
But with trust issues
And once she trusted you
Blind
Who can see the stiffness
In your smile
And to make it actual she'll be
Silly
But read between your tricky lines
And still, play it dumb
She's so confusing, hun

From smiling at the sliding screen at the ends of a fairy-tale
She found herself smiling at the castle falling apart
Shaking her head for it was what she thought
And she was right, like always
From expectations, then dealing with hur-
ricanes of disappointments
She was now already scheduling how to deal with them
Expecting the worst, like always
From Disney to life, it took her a while
From pink to black, the journey of a lost chameleon
But here she is now
From once upon a time to just another day
Just another night
And life went on...

Let her be
What she's scared of
The demon that ripped her wings
The witches who laughed
The goblins that threw rocks
On the fragile glass as it cracked
Let her say
What she's heard
Disguised sweetness
Formed as curse
Hidden meanings
Behind every wicked word
Let the wounded princess
Set fire
All this kingdom
And her delicate desires
No more wishes
No more dreams
A nightmare
Only she used to see
Let these be her
Let her be she
Let her be me

Is she in love?
Or is it merely the violin crying love in her ears
Is it telepathy?
Or merely her talking to herself
Does he smile more often?
Does everything remind him of someone?
Is it about to last forever?
No idea why but nothing seems to matter
Every flaw pins down to her disasters
But darling, she peeks over them
Why?

Just wants to lay her head
To breathe and believe again
A false hope would be good
For all the things she never could
Fool her with a lie
Another one
To cope with time
Till it's dawn
She'll stand up once more
And carry on

Perhaps it was a lovely love story
Exactly like in the movies
She, the princess
He, the Prince Charming
But instead of the cinemas
It played in her head
It was hard not to believe
And it's harder to not believe it
Merely a dream
And she woke up again

Oh, she's strong
She's faked smiles
Her heart turning into ashes
She wept when she was alone
Said words softly
And was stabbed very deep
No one noticed
Those kinds of cuts never bleed

She keeps her emotions
Distant from herself
Let alone...
Everybody else

Troubled eyes I see
Sweet words I hear
A broken soul I meet
Builds every soul in near
A shaky voice speaks
Yet, says strong words with no fear
Bags under her eyes
But a charming smile
Her lips like the deserts
But a face full of tears

They made her secret diary
Their rough copy
And her open heart
Their garage

Sing of sadness
And she's your passionate listener
Speak of heartbreaks
So she can turn them into poetry
Get creative
By not uttering a word
Tell her all
Tell her you're haunted
She may know your demon
From distant wars
It'll glide you on its shadowed wings
And from there
You'll freefall
Cry before her eyes
Your tears will lead her to streams
From there to drained halls
Of your arid heart
Grab shovels
She'll give rise to flumes
And you wreck her guarded walls

Sometimes she's the bloom
Her petals form to a maze
Of flowing love adorned with dew
Of curving hope wrapping you
Not holding back
Nor afraid too
Sometimes the seeds
Sprinkling remarks
Of wishes and daydreams
Of a million possibilities
Not resisting
Nor self-pitying
Sometimes the falling leaf
Wild and free
Making the fleeting fly
Worth her grounding life
But today she was the thorn
And she tore
All

Can you love the empty cage where once was a heart?
Or bear her clammy hand's touch
Can you understand the silence?
That's her soul's tongue
Can you lurk in the shadows, on a sunny day?
Or stroll under the rain, welcome every drop with a hug
Can you disgrace the rainbows for a dark sky?
That's her, hun
Or feel the rustling leaves, the wind,
the book, the lifeless rug?
Can you catch her at times when she'll run?
Or stop for ages beside her for a single turn
Tell me, can you?
If you say, you love

Pools of honey I see in her eyes
As sun rays dive deep into them
The sparkling stars light up her eyes
As tears hold back into them

Bring her silver chains
Wrap her up
Let them hug her
Then say it all
She won't shake
And you won't know
She is weak
Bring her silky scarf
Blind her eyes
Hurt her good
She won't try
To hide her face
And you won't know
She is crying
Bring her scented flowers
Dig a grave
Let it caress her
She won't persist
And you won't know
She is already dead
Do her a favour
Pretend she is strong
Before you begin

She used to be a princess waiting for her prince
Then she realised it wasn't a Disney
movie, no fairytales to live
She fought but lost, she was on her knees
All she got was lies, betrayal, and was cheated
Her life so evil—merciless, indiscreet,
unbearable scenarios it repeated
This wasn't the way she should've been treated
So she became a monster, no beauty, she was a Beast
Demons lived inside her, whispering in her ears
She knew this wasn't her
It was something of what she had a fear
With a growling voice she screamed
All she did was violence, and ruin peace
No one to understand, no one to wipe her tears
She set herself apart, letting no one near
It was her days of dark but after a while
The darkness became so dear

Maybe she's crazy now
And all that is said is true
She lost her mind
And constantly loses
She never understood
And she's always confused
She runs away from herself
Just to end up again and muse
She's an honest saint to her mind
But she lies to you
Maybe she's crazy now
And all that is said is true

She pretends to be free while reaping her invisible wings
She decorates her cage with hued butterflies
She explains who she is, barely what they want her to be
Like a puppet attached to its strings
She fools around, but she's alive at night
Think of her as you will, no one gets her anyway
I suppose this is the drill
A strange story, just another day...

Of course
You'll make it, sweetheart
But
Just a little broken
Less naive though
Just a little numb
Less endeavouring though
Just a little hopeless
Less disappointed though
Just a little sombre
Less fake smiling though
Just a little detached
Fewer feelings though
But isn't that freedom
And isn't that a life sentence
Of course
You'll make it

She feels small
Smaller than that tiny dot, she used to draw as rains
She now walks
But crawls under her skin, must not complain
She can talk
No longer trying too hard, clear and loud
Words are polished, repeating in doubts
Now she's tall
To climb all those walls, she's built for herself
Not letting in, it's a horrible place
She, herself wants to escape
Now that she has all the reasons to stay strong
She feels so damn small

Don't give her wings
She's mending her own through time
Don't tell her where to go
She's bound to the same sky as you are
But she's the one learning to fly
Yes, she has her head upon the clouds
She wants to pass through them now
Higher...

This can't be her
Do they know it too?
Or they only look at faces
Somebody change this
Bring her back
I've lost her track
She looked me in the eyes
And said...
Breathing
Feels redundant
Healing
Is so damn reluctant
I need to suffer
To know where hurts
I need to bleed
To find the cuts
Give me a break
Before I take
Every single will
Drift off for those hills
Where the bridges burn
And I won't turn
I'll live by the memories
Of those who'll then scorn me
Do me a favour and forget
It kills me to be a regret
Please, don't wait

Is what she said

She lies
So does her smile
So does her puzzled life
To herself
To her heart
And to God
Words so certain
Even she believes them
She's not hurting
Better off pretending
What once was a purpose
Now feels like a burden
She feels like a burden
Fond of hopeless desires
She's such an honest liar

She holds back
A sudden realisation
When she feels the cracks
Then you'll hear nothing but hesitations
And it's sad 'cause there's no use to being patient
Perhaps this is the way she'll be forever
Walking on eggshells even with herself
Constantly in lack
The girl with no reputation

بهار ما خزان یک روز خواهد شد

گلوی ما چو بی آواز که شاید شد

نصیب ما کند مرگ شوم یک سو در گوشه ای

ولی دنیا مرا از یاد خواهد شد

غنی آمد گدا آمد هزار پادشاه دور خود

که رفتند خاک گردیدند و باید شد

نمی دانم چرا ترسم ز مرگ خویش

اگر ترسم اگر خواهم ولی یک روز باید شد

هزاران جلوه ها آمد برفتند باز نگردیدن

تو ای خاموش نباشی معجزه این کار باید شد

Naive
Notions

If tomorrow starts without me
The sun won't even notice
But the moon will lose a lover
And the stars some lonesome wish
If tomorrow starts without me
The streets won't miss my shadow
But the walls would want to hear
Sighs, giggles, and silent tears
If tomorrow starts without me
The eyes won't discern
But a heart might sink
And late love shall be earned
If tomorrow starts without me
Anywise spinning
Estranged world

Wouldn't it be lovely
To be lovely in your eyes
To be your one and only
And the reason for your timid smile
To be your first thought in the morning
And the guardian of your dusky nights
To be the perfect piece that unravels your troubled mind
To be the mirror you rambled to, as a giggly free child
To be your never-ending path, and the
amble to nowhere till twilight
To be a happily ever after
You and I
Wouldn't it be lovely
To be lovely in your eyes

If she fell asleep
And had a beautiful dream
Running on the mile
A place you have never seen
And if she decided
To stay a little longer
Please don't wake her up
Don't wake her up
Because she won't
If you had to cry
Shed tears of joy
Of how she's finally living the life
Castaway where feels like home
Alone but at last not forlorn
If you had to come by
She's not under those plunged flowers
She's not boxed under this sky
Seek her in the stars
She'll be falling from one to another at nights
If you had to remember
Recall to bypass
Smiley clicks but not happy
Many familiar faces, no one to know
Don't gaze at seized moments, they passed
And if you had to meet
She'll be waiting for you
But please don't wake her up nor weep
It'll be beautiful
And she wouldn't want to leave

I saw a hummingbird
Pretty pretty wings
Beautiful beautiful voice
Amidst thin air, I saw it swim

Whirling and twirling
Across the stagnant flower
Which gazed at it in awe
Enduring useless powers

Its eyes caught the quiet
Cursed by vibrant hues
Espied in a fragile moment
And they both knew

Its ephemeral, uncertain soul
Consumed by delicate touch
But one can only live
For what it is conditioned

A hopeless thing
That didn't even cower
I saw a hummingbird
And a dying flower

There are versions
Of you and me
You're scared I'll change
I'm scared you've changed
Becoming what we don't know
Pretending we know well
That no one is appalled
To speak, to be themselves
We lived it ourselves
Yet know nothing at all
There are phases
We can only go through
You can't stay hardened
While melting
I can't be soft
With growing thorns
There are versions
All we can do is become them

        And still be ourselves

The fear of being misunderstood
ruins the possibility of ever being understood...

There's a string attached to each heart
It yanks in the breeze
In the rustling of trees
When eyes are closed
Yet, they start to see
As the chills scatter in your bones
You start to feel
There's a string...

Maybe she'll fall in love
If you tell her first
Why she sees her crying
Where once he made her laugh
Maybe she'll fall in love
If you show her first
The day he fell out of lust
And still chose to be hers
Maybe she'll fall in love
If you take her first
To her deformed heart
Where he's weaving
Maybe she'll fall in love
If she quit daydreaming
And fell in reality
If she dared to face the hurt
Maybe she'll fall in love

New pages were once tempting
Couldn't wait to ink
Sacred blood and secrets
And they were voiced
But never listened
Skimmed
And never heard
But the ink must've bled
And the words must've lined
Without being read
Which made them brave
Then they wrote for themselves
Hoping to never be understood
And never be felt

Oh, my dear
Who were the devils
That turned you into one
This skin doesn't suit your flesh
The fire you burst out
Burns nobody but you
Devils don't have hearts
But I hear a beat when you're close
To hell with hell
You're not its favourable host
Be my guest
For a change

You fear the fate
Or do you read it like a fiction?
Didn't like the ending
Nor the start
So you just stop
And throw that book in water
A getaway you thought
It reaches her, dancing in the shore
Standing out, familiar to her soul
She gets her light through the moon
Sparkling the pages in silver and light blue
Her ink, overflowing emotions
Music to her ears crashes of the ocean
And her audience is the stars above
Watching her muse with so much love
Lost is her home
Chaotic is her forms
Wrote nothing but lonely
Suddenly, now it's your favourite story

Your wrecked self trying to feel anew
Is like a burning rose adorned with dew
If the fire is put out
The rusting figure shall collapse
The drop of water
Gives audacity to hesitant hands
A sight of wild emotions
In that single drop
Is secured the oceans
From a distance
Watch it burn in motion

Will you hold on till it burns you
Or you're too cold to feel anything...?

Weary so is this hour
Both are hushed
I fall back and it stops
I stare at the wall
It goes on
Tick Tock
Into the abandoned moments
We are gushed
Seconds, minutes, clocks
Racing so is this heart
We are lost in niches
And are caught off guard
Telepathy, or going insane
Somehow, someone talks
Some nights I do too
This time I only eavesdrop
And we are hushed
Till dawn

Today
Before you say a word
Let her sing you songs
Of how every word
Won't mean a thing
When you break her heart
Tomorrow
Before you hold her hand
Let her make you feel its scars
Granted by unbidden wars
She still doubts
She has overcome
Yesterday
Before you said your hello
She wrote down her farewell
To herself
So it wouldn't hurt
When you go
Everyday
Begins in fear
You'll get to know her
Regret her
And hate her to death
Forevermore

Two broken hearts could never heal
Wounds need a Band-Aid
Not more pain to seep
Tired eyes need rest
Not reasons to weep
All this I do not know
Let's blame it on destiny

Cry underwater, free your tears
You won't complain there's no one to wipe
Since what they see is a smile ear to ear
Scream too, if you have to
Don't worry, no one will hear
Think about it all at once
Find something you still fear
If you don't, then you have nothing to lose
And that scares me, dear

The farther she goes
The less she sees
Shrinking figures, but then she sees it all at once
To not see anything
She ends up seeing everything
And to not feel for a sec
There she lies pondering on the bed
To not care, she doesn't care
And hence she ends up caring even more
What shall she do, for nothing seems to be in one's power?

Wish I could know what your pain is...
The reason behind that guarded heart
Those sacred tears I never get to see
Your half-smile fades, it's incomplete
Your words are so cautious
They shy away, each letter disguised as perfection
Formed as timid, as scared as your pain

I want to be a writer
Not being known as a writer
Just someone
Bleeding words
I want to write my heart out
But don't want you to read it
Read it as just something
And not my heart
I want to write good poems
I've gotten better
Since ink isn't the only thing
Staining papers
But don't you dare
Notice

In the garden of bowing roses, be a wildflower

—said by a wallflower

Fascinated by the fire
She didn't notice she was burning
Passing through just one time
That ended being what she kept doing
Swivelling on her stage
Melting together in rage
She was the dancing fairy

Too beautiful to put out

It'll pass
But, I will stay
A little bit of something
It'll take away
Will cost later
I'm afraid
The sun will rise
A new day awaits
Sights got used to shade
I know
It'll pass
The problem is
I will stay
Half-heartedly

Would it make a difference if tonight
I wrote the saddest poem?
Will it reach the one looking for their era's perfect poem?
Where would it hit the broken,
which piece will come to life for a moment?
As a form of a breeze, will it give air
to the one yearning to breathe?
As a form of a long hug
For the one caressing themselves to sleep
Will it be the hands wrapped around the trembling?
Confiding the dawn is near, to the sculptures of fear
Displayed as the dream better than what was seen so far
As the memory remembered to forget
the nightmare one can't wake up from
Will it be a tear in the eyes of the numb, to make him feel
Will the pain engraved amidst words be enough?
I wonder what'll happen to the void homes
If I could write the perfect poem

The wind turned the faces of the
timid flowers towards the sun
Just before the storm ripped them apart

She's spent staring at the broken pieces,
wondering if it'll ever be as it was
She'll spend the rest searching for a way to fix
it, then at least she could say that she tried

To shatter is not always tragic
A dandelion shattered to pieces
Blown away by a wind
Not by its will
How ironic
Hears a wistful wish
Sacred words safe inside its seeds
Now it travels the world, living its legacy
A dandelion broke free
Freed at last

I am walking with it, hand in hand, with no sense of touch. Staring at my tightened fist, holding on to the ghost that lives on. Who failed whom, I can't tell. This mirage is anchored to my fleeting self, and I'm looking for a chance to escape, thinking of nothing but getaways. I hope to be forgotten to get away with it, but then it hurts to know I am a regret.

We keep walking.

We're nothing but voids, trying to get a grasp of reality. And I'm trying my best to appear whole through broken windows all around me. One can lie by saying they like being invisible while knowing the truth that no one could ever see. Some see right through me, and it brings me ease. I hope I'm not the immortal, passing through, but then it hurts to know I am the living dead, waiting for it to get authorized.

We keep walking.

The route upheavals into a surge and then it comes in waves. Even if I'm at the shore, all I can see is it comes in waves. Even if it will never get close, all I can think of is the waves. Even if I will not drown, all I can breathe is the waves.

Even if I stand strong and tall. It comes in waves. I hope I am not here just to drown, but it hurts to stay afloat over prickling tides.

We keep walking.

It began in the middle of nowhere. But I remember being in happy Edens before. Little feet over pedals, running off to what I thought was better heaven. Deja vu.

Now, we are cautiously leading each other. It doesn't matter how carefully one takes their steps when hell is the destination. I hope I am not the devil, but it hurts to not know my crime, and hate myself like a criminal.

We keep walking.

Here's to the day I feel this estranged life's touch, trying to get familiar as we wander with each other through bullets and blood. And I hope I'm as wrong as it can get about what I'm discerning at the end of this thoroughfare. Perhaps there's something worth it behind that mountain about to be climbed.

We keep walking.

// Estranged Companion

طفلک آمد به دنیا نامکش بود جان عزیز

مثل نامش در دل ما بود صد بار چون عزیز

او که افغان کوچه کابل بود در مغز شهر

بعد جوان گردید و از خود داشت فرزند عزیز

با هزار عیش و نعمت کرد کلان، آن هر یکی

رو به پیری میرود هر کی دور گردد عزیز

هر کی ماستر گشت انجینیر طریق خویش را

وای از این تحصیل چی داد آخر برای آن عزیز

این چی رسمیست در جهان دادند گران آن پیر را

خوب خلاصه درد سر دادن ترا ای دوست گردید فوت عزیز

بعد ز مرگش ختم نان گاو و گوسفند شد حلال

چون که ما داریم شریک و سیال و عزیز

ای خاموش کردی بیان آخر تو دردی خویش را

هر کی دارد طفل در پیری کند یا رب عزیز

Hostage

I'll set my soul free
Even when I'm trapped
Oh, I'll sing inside my cell
All the happy songs that I've never had
There will be a window
A ray of light will find its way in rad
The shadow of the bars will fall beautifully on the floor
All I see is art, in my pain, in this
place, in my broken laughs
The way the walls will crumble
Will make it up for the paint
The songbirds will sing
And I will carve their words, yet again
I've set my soul free, even if I'm trapped

There's a wave
And it's there
Right in front of you
Never letting you in
Always there to be seen
To drown seems awful
And to live in dismay
Is tasting death bit by bit
There's a wave
I can see it

A certain type of tiredness is spreading in her bones
She has a longing for the casket to be her safe home
A certain type of truth is breathing in her nerves
The realization born with each drag hurts
A certain type of loss is winning her over
She's running out of white flags moreover
A certain type of hell she's latched in
And she keeps searching for her sin

Hush
Let's speak our language
Letters we invented through experience
Scared, sacred words we understand
Let's talk silence
We know it best

I see my reflection
Now I can't decide
Is it me lacking affection?
Or is it just your sad eyes

They are coming
It is coming
Now it feels like
You're also coming
After me
I'm running
I'm running
Now it feels like
I'm running
After me
If it's a nightmare
Pinching isn't working
There's no chasm to fall
After me
My voice is tamed
From all the screams
You're just crying
After me
Doesn't it hurt you
Watching me suffer
Please wake me up
Everything is coming
After me

No time...
Can't stop the ticker, even if I broke it,
another will be there, counting
Don't want to stop it, even if I did
Somewhere within there are always demons
running late, haunting
No time to live, no time to die, just give me a sec
So dead inside, crawling
What are you, my dear?
Something I possess?
Then why is it always you I'm desperately wanting?
You're never enough, yet too much to bear
In fears of wasting you,
I get wasted myself, there you are then, taunting
I owe you my life, perhaps to have a life later,
but here you are, daunting
No time to explain, shrugged it off with a smile
No time to feel, can't stay up all night,
how to face the sun with tired eyes?
I get I'll never be good enough, please stop flaunting
And at the end, all they say is, there's no such thing as time
Not during the numbers, you're entitled to now
And all I can say is
I loathe our bonding

Play a song
Till the dawn
Or else
My mind will sing me one
A horrible taste
Has no grace
Will tear me down
Till dusk

What is this, my love?
Such agony
Why are we going through this?
When there is no way to go through
For you to be here
And for me to be there
For us to be anywhere
What is this, my love?

There's a force
Pulls me down
Deeper
All the way to nowhere
Have you ever been there?
Everything is like it was
But I just don't see
Hear honest voices
Don't know what a word means
Cherry picking thoughts to remain there
Too lethargic to feel
A journey to nowhere

It's falling
You
Me
The world
Don't know where
Don't know why
But this falling
Will be the reason for a rise
When it's time
Rise again

When it doesn't feel right
Wonder what people do...
Do they have the tongue of the bolds?
The hearts that can handily hold
The weight of the world
Do they have ears nearby?
Listening to silent cries
Daring honesty, simple life
Do they have hope?
Not just vivid words
But a firm grip to a tightrope
Strong intentions to not let go
Teach me, earnestly yours

Once at a time
Let's have a deal, dear life
If the day be like that
Fancy me a sweet dream at night
And if the night wasn't kind
Let there be a limelight
When it's time for people
Let me be there for myself
And when I'm breaking myself
Let someone hold me tight
If it's again my naiveness
Let the wrecking truths
Tear pretty lies
When the voices are too loud
Let the earphones sway high
If the world is collapsing
Let me escape to my universe for sometime
When we hating on each other
Let me fall in love with the ways I die
Once at a time
Dear life

A blank page...
A mystery for the bemused
Till they solve it for themselves
An answer for the conclusionist
They will end it right away
A mistake for the regretful
Wishing death upon themselves until it happens
A self-destructive ache for the over-thinker
An inheritance for life
Blank is obnoxious

If she died
If it stopped
And it rained
So you won't have to wipe your tears
And the sun rose the next day
Flowers bloomed so you won't have to bring them
Too young but, honestly had enough
Let her rest
Play her a song and go
The world will keep on spinning
There will be another one like her
Or maybe not
And maybe that's a good thing

You're drowning, but it's not in the water
It's something else
Deeper than the seas
No way to stay afloat
Can't get a hold on to something
You can breathe, but you're suffocating
You're still, but fighting for your life
You're drowning, in nothingness

Amidst ebony waves
Under ebony skies
Over ebony voids
I'm afloat
In this serene gloom
Air is not breathed
Universe is dead
I'm afloat
Abyss can't drown
There is no shore
In this nothingness
I'm afloat

Empty
Nothing forms out of this loathed tongue
No words make sense
No letters convey what one wants to say, I'm done
Empty
Mistrusting each sense
Shutting each thought, chaotic mind
No sense ever made sense
And no whisper was ever kind
Empty
If only it could empty too
Every single thing between cages
Set as ribs just to
Calm the wild when it rages
Empty
Overflowing with so much emptiness

Let me escape this misery
These walls won't let me go
The wind whispers stories
From the other side of the world
Yet the silence has this wisdom
I will never know
Life tries to teach me a lesson
In a language I can't understand
I can see the door wide open
But these walls won't let me go

The walls that have imprisoned
Are the only ones who listen
Hours of silence, classical music, words that are never said
Random giggles, endless sighs, awaken nights, hollow days
Tall enough to block the view
They whisper
"There's nothing new
It's the same old stories happening
You stay inside or else you'll be rambling
Again..."

Don't you want to skydive?
From the towering walls
You've built for yourself
Each brick the result of a bitter experience
Flip backwards and plunge
All that you've gone through is not your fault
Free a hostage and do yourself a favour
Skydive with me
Make yourself your saviour

Eventually, their screams turned to
gentle lulls, their scorns into soft music,
And she danced her way out of their hell

ای دیر زمان، ظلم زمان را تو به سیری و صبوری

ای خاک کهن، کوه چمن شاهد هر درد نمودی

زاهد نظران محو تماشایی کجایید

از دست رویم خاک به سر همچو گدا بر سری شوری

شاید نرسد فرصتت ای دست چو فردا

امروز تو بیا دست ستم گیر که هر چند به دوری

کج منزل آباد تو را نیست بقایی

ای یزد زمان آیی و گوی که پشیمان چو موری

خاموش تو بدان لطف زمان را مکن ناله بسیار

آن شاه زمان گنج جهان را همه یک روز به گوری

Many routes
No destination
Many destinations
But no route
A complete cycle
Of grim histories
Hopeful futures
But a broken cycle
Ivory pages
Tired hands
Crimson papers
But torn veins
Senseless aches
Endless discovering
No point of view
But meaningful tragedies
Beckoning stares
Memorized names
Familiar faces
But alienated feelings
Life's been a contradiction
And I another paradox

In my conceptual universe
Letters orbit the heart
And this flaming core
Gravitates frigid words
To cool down
In my conceptual universe
Chasms teleport to endless chases
Dwelling from one void to the other
Won't grant time-travelling
Nothing's functioning in the present
In my conceptual universe
There's nothing but empty spaces
I consume it to pay the wages
I'm a floating astronaut
Who doesn't want to go home

My room is my safe haven
But sometimes, the world is tempting
My ceiling is my galaxy
But sometimes those stars voice my name
My playlists are my best buddies
But sometimes, some people sound sweeter
My pessimistic self is my saviour
But I still am a believer
All I can say...
I hate this world a little bit more
But I fall in love with it every day

I want to write soaring sunrise
But who will bear the silence after dusk?
The lonely blossoms endeavouring
Woes of the morning at night alters them to rust
I want to write songbirds descant
But who will listen to the quiet?
Gazing into the abyss, yearning to rant
I want to write about moonlight dancing
Chocolate and heart-shaped fancies
But who will heal the broken heart?
Ashes of oneself are all they got
I want to write wheezing giggles, my dear
But who will wipe that shedding tear
Free falling on its own
Drying and going cold
You read happy
But they have sorrow
To relate I will write
Their pains I will borrow

If I was a flower and I was picked
I wonder...
Would it be for what I was
Or just a temptation to give it a try?
A reason for an ungrateful smile
Which caused my life
"Thank you"
And I'm inhaled for a second
Already done, and there I lie
Inside a lonely vase
Looking at them dancing
As they forget
I still exist
For a little while

I've been too far away
From flesh and bones
Who assume we're very close
I'm a hunter of wandering souls
Who don't even exist
In love with ghosts

Far away
From fun and laughter
Just to disguise disasters
Your deepest sorrows
Is what I'm after

Far away
From comfortable arts
Lovers and happy hearts
Your broken pieces
Top my charts

Far away
From everything and everyone
The daylight and its pretty sun
Luna and her scars
Bestow my warm distant hugs

And I've always been
A little too far away
Even from myself

If it stopped writing
Write poems about love
Happy endings and hope
Write my name at a corner
Burn the papers
Locked in folders
Or read at your own risk
Don't you dare feel them
Please don't tell them
Who I was

If it stopped beating
The music will guide you
To where you'll find me
Collect hues of happiness
Say I was overflowing with it
Share a radiant
Of the painted walls
Please don't tell them
Where I was

If it stopped feeling
Know it's at peace
Resting and healing
Shut the ghostly chambers
Let the wraiths live

If one said
I've been something to someone
Please don't tell them
What I was
If it stopped
Once upon a weary heart

To make words with no need to struggle with what it would mean to anyone, forgetting if it means anything at all. Busy painting in another head, leaving oneself's colourless, paving predictable routes while wishing to get lost.

Nonsense would mean something sense could never, splashing buckets of hues, camouflaging deformed pages that are easy to rip and set free. Running on the skies, driving on the clouds, reaching implicit destiny.

Nothingness could be none could have, while having it ever, living it eternal, denying it forever. Thinking in words and feeling in silence, damned ways of sentients. Where easy is a habit overwhelmingly making it harder, in the lands of mad beings the madness could be smarter.

They may call it
A senseless wanderer's confession
Nonsense and nothingness

How to make them understand
That they will never really understand
There's no need to amend
Words can't convey
A living contradiction
Doesn't make sense
How to make you understand
That you'd never know who I am

It unnerves me when I can't imagine
'Cause when I can't imagine
I cannot write
And when I cannot write
I can't breathe looking at the sluggish void
Where letters are supposed to dance
To melancholic melodies
Rhyme to the beats of teardrops falling
Mimicking memories
So they won't be forgotten
Without them, who am I?
My imagination,
I'd rather lose my senses to you
Than lose myself in your want
In this frantic presence
Be my wondrous time machine
In this lonesome reality
Be my infinite ally

If I could make it quieter
Would you hear my heartbeat
Outrunning seconds
Hauling weight you can't see
Would you hear my thoughts
While taking a step back
And desire to run away
To distance from a maniac
Would you hear lumps
Running down my throat
They voice themselves that way
The swallowed words
If I could make it quieter
I could speak for myself
And brace without shaking
For another farewell

You withdraw from gleaming rainbows
They don't last long
You match your devoted dusks
Lulling you to your nightmares
So you can be grateful for your days
You love to be hated
You'll make sure
To be left alone
You escape sweet dreams
They mess with your sanity
And then you err to differentiate
The reality
Nearing a gloomy villa
You mimic the thunder
And drink its tears
What if you're the villain?

Have you ever mourned the living
And pity the breaths
Picked one fresh flower that smells of petrichor
Gently let it pass through your skull
Wrote with the ink of its bleeding thorns
Joyously composed poems of endings
And carved them on stranger's graveyards
Danced your way out
Wrapped in withering self
Have you ever mourned the living
And celebrated death

Before the war started, I fought so much
now I can't raise my hand
Guns are aimed, they are armed,
waiting for them to pull the trigger so I could finally land
Before you said a word, I heard so much
now even silence scares me to death
If you ever fancied a conflict,
hail your victory, there's no stamina left
Before it happens, it's already happened a thousand times
now when it happened nothing matters
Oh, I miss the times,
there was an amicable soul inside and I truly had her
Before getting in, I find my way out
to end up alone at least in a familiar place.
Dug a hole there too, just in case
Before it fell, I had kissed it farewell,
didn't know I had it until it was gone
And before the dusk, I start to loathe the sun,
so it's only my fault
Before the race, I've won it already,
none could ever run away as fast as I can
At the final touches, I rip off the page,
peaky sheet emerges, and that is all I've ever had

Did you know?
Nobody knows you
How can one
When you pretend you don't either
What's the fun of knowing?
Let's play the fools
Call it flaws
And not triggers
Call it virtue
And not trauma
Call it labels
And not camouflage
Call it mature
And not sick
Anyone they'll like you to be
Any way they'll like you to be
Let's pretend
This world is a classic play
You be happy
I'll be laughing
And when it's done
Let's wither
Behind the scenes
Did you know?
Nobody knows you

What if I told you
I'm just like everyone else
Trying to be somebody
In estranged self
What will you do
When you found
My drastic flaws
Standing out
What if I told you
I wear black
Mourning the living
And celebrating death
What will you do
To know all you could
While I fear
Being understood
What if I told you
I'm still lurking
To make a broken thing
Start working
What if I told you
I'm just like everyone else
But trying to be somebody
In estranged self

There's a walking corpse
Living on its tears
Dying by its fears
Breathing as a habit
Tasteless air
Sleeping in a casket
Vivid nightmares
But if it stares into the darkness for too long
It become its shadow
Following where it led
From nothingness to nothingness
Chasms to chasms
Voids to voids
They keep walking
Hand in hand
Till they are one
And no one

I'm sick of the darkness
But, oh, don't I write so well in the gloom
The letters come to me and I don't have to suffer
In finding the fancy way to disguise
The last thing I'll care about will be rhyme
How ironic
I'll be more blunt than the devil in your head
It will scare away
I will use I
And I will use you
No obscuring points of view
How ironic
Is the darkness

The days are passing by me
And I'm not even there
Where am I?
I can't tell
Some days I have the map
And I start to believe on paved tracks
That they won't lead me wrong
Some days I tear it myself
Search for the worst route
And run to get lost
Then the days pass by me
And I'm not even there

Smile as much as you can hold
At them
Laugh as much as you can tolerate
With them
Talk as much as you can take
Small talks
Give as much as they can reciprocate
Your heavy heart
But don't you dare
Do any of these
In front of me

Are things born like that
Or they do it to themselves
I can't be born
With a broken heart
But then why can't I tell
Who broke it
You can't be born with endless tears
But then why
They can't seem to run out
You don't tire
Of crying to the walls
And walls don't tire
Watching you fall apart
I can't be born with a silent tongue
With a deafening mind
I try to speak for once
Yet I choke into words
And hope they'll just know
You can't wait to runaway
But then why
You're chasing yourself
We weren't born like that

If I held my tongue
I won't be in trouble
All this chatter asks for something
I no longer have
So I let words speak for me
And they write of hope
While shaking themselves
They compose of colossal cosmos
But feel so small
Then highlight endless odds
But the weary words are lining
Searching for happy endings
In dreary tales
And they write of courage
While hiding behind metaphors
In damaged letters
They inscribe about love and faith
Don't call them hypocrite
Words are trying somehow
But they should've been brave by now
I should've been brave by now

But this fear
That I'll choke into words
Yet won't know what to say
And it will keep playing in my head
Or say the wrong words
Maybe exactly what I wasn't supposed to say
Or worse, my truth
But this fear
That I'll write letters
Send to wrong addresses
And it will be used as heart-breaking for dummies
Or a joke that's not even funny
Maybe a poem on how not to love
Or worse, how not to write
But this fear that I won't ever believe in words
This fear never fades away

How to be free?
When your skin is what has wrapped your tired self
When your ribs are the cage
Your feral heart another captive
You're nothing but a hostage
Who's built the vault in hopes to save
God knows what
How to be free when each bar is rooted from rigid yore
You keep weaving more
How to be free?
When shadows display wings
So you keep staring at the walls
How to be free?
You're the prison
You're the captive
You're the key

Break her a little
She's letting you in
It needs to get out
There's something within
It hits the walls
Her bones break and spin
It screams
Echoes in her mind
It's wild
Shedding young skin
She had to track it down
And burn its wings
Just to make it limp
But she has to let it go
Break her a little

She's letting you in

What if I ran out of words...?
No more rambling
No more seeping rough copies
No more headless pens
No more retreat from gatherings
No more lonesome hobbies
No more late-night amends
Wish I could run out of words...

I'm a criminal
In search for my crime
To find solace
And stop charging life
I'm in prison
Build before its key
Caressing each bar
Reminiscing distant memories
I'm a lover
In search of faith
That they truly make it
And hearts don't break
I'm a writer
With broken hands
And running soles
Endeavouring to enhance

Memorized niches
I know the ceiling by heart
Each little imperfection
And its bothersome scars
The curtains aren't stagnant at all
If you stare at them long enough
They breathe out delicate winds
Which ends up as a subtle touch
The distinct voices of strangers
And the crickets never shut up
Silence gets obnoxious
Thankfully, music has my love
Passionately devouring the nightlife
Severe observations
And the room stares back
As I write my hallucinations

I want to touch
The air we're caught up in
The glistening light following me
The waves of fragile voices I can only hear
It can't be hearing
The heart craving to race
I want to touch
The silence and dig out words
The soul in the essence of a scared ghost
The things no one could get through
I want to touch...
The untouchables

Anxious for where we stand
We forgot where we were before
Where we once stood
Then only hope to seek the slightest space somewhere
That's when we're doomed, that's when we shrink to fit in
Lurking in the corners of unrequited spaces
Hoping to be enough
But how can you be enough, where you cannot even move?
Let alone bloom...
Dear, get out
You deserve a heart as spacious as yours
A love, as deep as your soul

If only I could be you
I wonder
How would it be to live in a world like today
And yet, not feel
To not get down by a stranger's sigh
To never read between the lines
To not get trapped in others body
But be the owner of my emotions
To not die in order to heal
To have a wounded soul eventually set free

Searching for reasons to write again
Every breath sums up as debt if I don't
As the sun sets, the urge arises
An elusive force I can't ignore
Oddly enough, by recalling my pieces
I feel whole
A debate to feel or not, as if I'm in control
Gamble of memories, rummaging of words
Cultivates her
Silly girl, trying to save the world

I don't forget that easily
Sometimes it's a blessing
Sometimes it's a curse
But you'll be remembered as a blessing
Always

If I am to drown
I shall drown in rosy sunsets, along with my source of light
If I am to die
I shall die in joy as the happy child will pick
me up from the gardens, all smiles
If I am to fall
I shall fall in nightlife to give rise to a wish
that has been broken many times
I will not leave as me,
but in essence that carries glee to thee

To know my place in every life
I wonder then, what I'd be like
Listen to every time my name is called
Is it whispered in any heart?
Sync with a heartbeat, feel what it feels
Believe words are meant
No longer lethargic to make a friend
To know my place in every life
I wonder then, what I'd be like...

I'll be ok among purple tulips, fragmenting my aura
I've lost my senses
I'll be ok under the thunderous sky, retrieving my feelings
Sick of my defences
I'll be ok besides the collision of distant
waves, harmonizing with my sighs
The shore our fragile fences
I'll be ok in the wilderness, healing me
from the scrapes of the urban
Sophistication had its consequences
I'll be ok deep underwater, drowning all the shallowness
The eerie gloom will merge with sparkling, blue lenses
I'll be ok far, far away, forgetting my
name and being forgotten
Me and my lonesome condolences

فلک نگر تو ز تنگنا دل افسرده ما را

و ز بسی سوختن شمع چی باکی من و پیمانه ما را

نه قفس رهاندم از بند، نه دهر خواستم بر خویش

به چی فرجام رسد آخر دلی دیوانه مارا

نه عمر خضر وفا کرد، نه اسکندر بماند، نه ملک

من درویش چی دانم، چی بگویم حال و افسانه مارا

بس که دیدم ز زمان، زمان گری ها

ای خدا یا کفنم کن رهی کاشانه ما را

قفس سینه چی داند که هیولای زمانه

نه دهد مرگ و کشاند روی زولانه مارا

تو گشایی رهی مارا که چنان مور و خاموشیم

تو نمای گر از این بند ملالت رهی مارا

Hot Chocolate

The soft amber light behind the curtains
A sign of pouring burdens
That the sky is about to cry
To make things alright
For you and I

I adore the rain
Pours into my heart
Refills it
Its scent wakes me up from my nightmares
Taught me not to be afraid
To show my tears
So we can cry together

Raindrops just to be heard, you fall down
You leave your highest status, just to hit the ground
You fall, you flow
Yet they never noticed
For there is so much of you crashing around
Doesn't it hurt that you still fall for them?
 Or you've been used to letting yourself down?
Raindrops, everything between us...
Is a precise common ground

There's something so poetic about these falling leaves
Flowing by the gust
Like melancholic poets, yearning for stability
Lying to be crushed
Like the hopeless romantic, walked all over
Turns to dust
Like emotions poured into poems
For a truce between the expressive heart
And the wordy mind

Unpaved routes, wild yet fragile
Weeping willows, hued teardrops
Each freefalls and the wind murmured
This prey wishes, may its despair never halt

An open sky shying away, stealing glances
From behind the greenery crowns
Hoping not to be seen
While seeking to stand out
Smiling similarities
Estranged selves laughing
In this chaos of calmness
I was just a wanderer passing

It's here again
The desire to alter
Into those hued leaves
A fall worth the fly
Softly detaching
One last time
Gushed by a breeze
Amidst a farewell
And off it goes
Into the unknown
Till other regards
It's here again
The desire to alter
Into those brave drops
Free-falling from murky skies
Splashing pearls
Before my timid eyes
By gazing them
They too get bold
Till other storms
It's here again
May the steam of your tea
Dance to your serene harmony
The warmth from your hands
Reach your frigid heart
And if it's bound to happen
May this be your gentle fall

Snowflakes withering from the window
Cold tea on the kitchen table
Getting colder
Will it freeze now?
Any moment
But just seconds ago
Figures were elevating from it
Amidst the steam
Nostalgic scents faded
But just seconds ago
Brave hands would clasp
Any hand nearby
Not shoved in vacant spaces
Redeeming the numb
But just seconds ago
A blanket was here
Cartoonish and pink
Drenched gloves
In melting snowballs
But just seconds ago
Winter was my favourite
Snowflakes keep withering from the windows
It's getting colder and colder

Cold
It's winter but been perishing for this whole year
Should get used to, but the warm teases every now and then
Hold
It's hard to hold on, been on the verge, been so near
Should expect the worst but hope
Oh hope seizes every now and then
No
I don't know how it'll end
Nor when this hefty caravan is going to veer
Should stop, can't see the finish line, but the road
The road gets pretty
It eases every now and then

It's snowing
I'm watching from the window
How they gracefully hit the ground
Coming down from the highest
Somewhere we have never been
Made me realize, sometimes
Falling has its own
Benefits
Beauty
And reasons

You feel like a heavy blanket
On a snowy day
You melt the ache in the bones
With the cosy words that you say
Your warm existence is enough
For one to stay

Something's changing
Something's changed
It's not the red and brown hues
Nor the gentle, gloomy sky
Not the deserted trees in queues
Nor once a sunny day, now opening-up to cry
Not the heavyweight each carries
Withdrawal isn't for the hefty shoes
Nor the layers I tally, been undercover for a long time
It's not solely the season
That's changed for me and you

You'll catch them
Smiling across the sink
Fingers adorned with ink
Locked in silent rooms
Then watch them bloom
Must be a poet
Dreaming wide awake
Staring as you lay
Waiting for you to sleep
To write of how beautifully
Your lashes intertwine
And your lips shine
Of how they miss you
While being there with you
And how they long to tell
But they'll write instead...
Must be a poet
Struggling to have a voice
Telepathy their only choice
Don't be afraid to ask
Of heartbreaks pain and art

But let them overcome overthinking
In fear and doubt, they'll be sinking
Don't worry, they'll speak at last
Of what's hiding nether intimate scars
Must be a poet
A bit of a hypocrite
A great deal of a lunatic
Pledged they won't feel
Fell in love in a heartbeat...
Must be a poet
Adoring from afar
Wishing upon broken stars
With torn stuff, they're in tune
Ranting to the lonelier moon
Using her name in every muse
Boldly breaking rules
Setting new ones before the fall
Hiding behind rhyming walls
With words, they fill the void
Must be a poet

There's something about dawn
There's something about dusk
Perhaps it's the absence of existence
And the reconciliation with the stars
Or maybe it's the hued flavours
Of the rising sun

مرگ یعنی انتظار این و آن و بس دیگر

مرگ یعنی ختم بیم و ترس از هر خس دیگر

خوش به حال آن که کرد دنیای فانی را لبیک

درد گردون را نداند نی بسوزد نی از نا کس دیگر

ما امید خود بستیم بعد از این با مرگ خویش

چون که قدری تو بدانند بعد مرگ فرضی دیگر

زنده را تا زنده است ای وای عجب رنجش مدار

یک دو گفتار بود خاموش کرد ندانم بود تا درس دیگر

Amateur

I must learn the way you laugh loudly
So I don't hear your breaking heart
And the art of comforting words
You wished someone had said to you
Let me be your soft quiet

I must learn the way your eyes radiate
So the gloom in mine is scared away
But there's a flood behind yours
Awaiting darkness
Let me be the pillow that'll hide them

I must learn the way you detach
So I can connect to myself
And find you there
Caring from the corners
Let me be your distant Luna
In between phases
Let us hide away

Sometimes...something happens,
and all you can do is ask your soul,
"What is it you know that I don't..."

Will you wait for your response
While still holding the missive in your hands
Who dares to inscribe
When red ink is the demand
Perhaps paper cuts won't hurt much
If it lets you let it out
Be careful, my dear
Words might not but blood runs out
Will you still think of phrases
If empty letters are all you can send
Or your fluency in silence
Taught you how to amend
Dilating eyes are expanding
Doesn't your gaze tire
Or on that ivory chasm
Hallucinates all that you desire
Brainstorming for hours
Time is running faster
You can't stop smiling
Daydreaming about the answer
Sanity wreckers
Your unsent letters

Don't love her now
Save it
For when you'll loathe her name
See through her soul
Despise her face
And she wouldn't know
What to do
Don't promise her now
Save it
For when you'll regret the day
You found her
And the stars aligned
They will be falling apart
And she wouldn't know
What to do
Don't hold her hand now
Save it
For when you would want to let go
Of her pricking palms
She would want to run away
Then get lost
And she wouldn't know
What to do
Don't heal her heart now
Save it
For when you'd break it
She'd stare at its pieces
There's only one that she has
And she wouldn't know
What to do

If she was forever full
There wouldn't be a slide
That'll depart to vacant lull
How could one swing in motion
Amidst shooting stars and pull
Clasping from her crescent
If she was forever white
Where would all the blood fade away
That flood her with sins of might
As she bleeds with the living martyrs
Who yearn for that eerie night
While some hideaway
If she was forever there
The weight would make her fall
Unbearable sights to bear
Lest some only leave their room
To discern her somewhere
Till another full moon
If she was forever his
She wouldn't be held so dear
Seen through and never missed
Don't wreck the curse, fight the lust
Fly a true love's kiss
And hope it'll find her

Make her a wish
Blow on the dandelion
And let each seed rooted in your heart fly away
Make her a poem
You are too scared to write
End her with a full stop
 Let it be the only drop of ink on that blank page
Make her a rose
Gently descend your fingers
Let them bleed by the thorns
So you could throw away
Make her a lucid dream
In which you loathe her existence
Call it a nightmare when you're awake
Make her a memory you can't remember
An invisible portrait you tore
Surrender her to nothingness
Let her fade away
Make her your start only to end
Your almost that couldn't make it
Branded words in perishing lips
Things that are left unsaid

Maybe if we were honest
Those days would fall shorter
As we'd swim in evenfall
That'd be what we wanted
You'd scream
Not in your pillow
I won't ask why
Less scary
Than your forced smiles
And averting eyes
I'd say, "Tonight
No matter how much I try
I can only be sad
And that's alright"
You'd stop screaming
I'd stop redeeming
We'd begin daydreaming
In sheer silence
Watching the world fall apart
And we did our part
Maybe if we were honest
Days wouldn't feel like nights
And nights wouldn't be spent in regrets
Our disasters would be our solace
If only we were honest

I'll wear your shoes
And you wear mine
Let's go for a walk
The little stones bother, you're doing fine
I see you're not running
For uncommitted crimes
You're slowing down
As I begin to stride
Engulfed with foreign comfort
But, I don't mind
I find solace in this estrangement
These new pairs don't wanna run
You stop and tug your shoes
Each gravel falls out one by one
And I stand there startled
I was searching for ways to lessen the pain
While I could get rid of it all at once

This world has a beautiful view
But when you get closer
You start to see its ugliest sights
The most heartless creatures
And I fear
It has turned you like itself
A nightmare
Dressed as a daydream...

I see tears in colours
Restored in my depths
It's when I collect them
Whereas, I feel special
I hear desires from yore
Echoing within
I'm an attractive lure
Heartbroken my attachment
Heartbreakers my magnet
I feel lovers near me
For I am numb
From the past, a future I see
They'll come to me soon
Apiece, broken and bruised
Amidst turmoil, each will wish for peace
I'll sing of silence, reflect ample ebony
We'll dance in stillness, drown in shallow agony
Laughing children are spiralling
I'm the core of their joy
Each asks of so much
But I've lost my foy
You must have guessed it yet
I must be a wishing well

I don't have much to give
But I have some things
Like crumpled papers I hide
And can't throw away
I'm loaded with desires
But the will is hopeless
Silence and long-lasting sighs
Lull me to stay awake
But I have stories
That'll keep you up all night
And I'll make sure
You wouldn't want to stay
I collect wasted bullets
To kill them in my mind
I paint words with their blood
Petty poems I inscribe
I'm loaded with questions
But the trigger is broken
I'll lock myself in hell
And pray for you paradise
I ask no ease for pain
To have something to write
You can keep the flowers
I have thorns that survive
You can keep your heart
I got rid of mine
I'm loaded with love
But I feel so worthless
They're all ugly things
I don't have much to give
But, I'll happily give you my life

There's a silhouette dancing in the dark
With each step, he is outlined in purple
It makes him stand out
He flickers, flickers and flickers
There's music playing
It sounds as his laughs
But, when it stops
Is when he begins to weep
Then he swivels, swivels and swivels
Parading to his emotions, he asks for my hand
I want to hold, but it passes through
For I am the dark engulfing him
Barren and out of sight
Unbothered by each other's presence
Unaware of what we are
We shrivel, we shrivel and shrivel...

Fell in love with the little things
The way your voice heals
The way your smile lifts your cheeks
And the way your eyes shine slightly brighter
When they look at me

I've looked through eyes
And perceived their souls
Some deliberately innocent
Some brutally ice cold
A gaze utterly diligent
One living inside their own world
But, when I saw yours
I saw an angel from the skies
Something so much more
Certainly not just a soul

Have her when she's happy
Facing the sun in elegant turns
She's funny that way
Less complicated
More lovable
The way they always like
Applaud her in her bloom
Look away when it's raining
And it's forcing her to bow down
Less appealing
More miserable
Who even knows how to deal with it
Let her hide beneath the snow
When there's nothing left to show
Let her be
Let it grow
Let her go

Those eyes
That smile
The curls
That face
Like diamonds
Like heavens
Like silk
You're a treasure
So rare

Let me ink your pain in my blood
They won't find you again
They'll get engraved with me
Together we will turn to dust

Love you more than the stars in the galaxies
You made my life
Shine brighter than them

I'll hold your hand, pull you out of the darkness
You're about to get drowned
But, if I wasn't strong enough
Pull me inside your darkest thoughts and feels
We'll get lost together and never be found

Find her the fortune teller who makes one forget the past, an admirable mystery to think of, no more tasteless experiences, endlessly being experienced over and over again. Tell him to take all the time he needs, the visitor is not impatient, just a little tired they say

She will take the walk and stare at him talking about her with the gleam in his eyes, speaking of a bright future, better days, and the girl will smile, listening to familiar words and the rest she can almost predict, how ironic. Don't mind the anomaly running away, she will come back they say

Breathless, parched, and lost, but she will think of his words. A fair share of poison boiling in her throat, desperately in search of an antidote, fresh blood will drip from her lips, painted all over ivory teeth, she will smile widely while aimlessly dancing her way, it gets better they say

Find her the fortune teller, she has a bright future they say

Maybe it's not the heights
It's always been about the falling
Imagining it breaking into pieces
It's already a bit broken
Falling in nightmares
Never crashing makes it worse
The fear of falling for someone
I'm afraid
There's no safety net
Not a skydiver
I only know how to fall
Free falling
Into an endless chasm of fear of the falling itself
Maybe it's not the heights

Nowadays, everything feels like a replica. I swear these days are plagiarized from the estranged yesterdays. I think of things to write, but I end up writing the same story, written in different colours. If you combine them, they render to a blank page where once letters sailed, on their way to write happily ever afters. Or was it all over my head? They end up being nothing, coming down to nothingness. Not even a stain remains to remind me that someday, something was there.

I tried to make sense of it, but people don't believe in ghosts, and it lives in my head, mercilessly. They want proof, and I am not enough, never been. It's a scary wraith, living a scarier existence. Fear makes me do silly things, I can only hope they see it as ego. It doesn't exist and the past is dead they say, but then I wonder, how am I handed flowers, my days turned black, led to its graveyard, and then told not to grieve?

What do tears mean in a weeping world? What is pain to the numb? What is love to a broken heart? What are the means to escape in a spinning realm, running, running, running... There's only one answer, nothing. So wipe their tears and hail your dead heart.

Where to fall and have that euphoria making me feel something, without having to deal with the consequences of crashing?

Falling in the chasm, in a nightmare, for someone, is there a difference? I watch them ripping each other's existence from bones since none is seeing in the dark, there's no light in gloomy souls, each solely monuments of black holes. And I've tried to make sense, to not lose my senses, but it's just nothing. All I've ever known comes down to see-through words that cannot talk, and I'll call it

// Writer's Block

از کجا آغاز کنم ای چمن سرخگون من؟

در باغچه های وحشی تو، آهوی سرنگونم من

در رگ رگ درخت نو نهالت ریشه افتاده گیست

بگو ای ساکت، آن که اجدادت را بر افراشته کیست؟

ابر نه، غبار تاریست بر تو

باران نه، خون جاریست در تو

جوی های روان آن رام نه کرد تشنه ات را

از خانه خانه میچینند گل های سنگرت را

پر پر می شویم بر تو

مرده و غرس می شویم در تو

از کجا آغاز کنم ای چمن سرخگون من؟

یک شاهد خسته دیگری گردونت من

Permitted
Pessimist

The wind has a way
It has a way
Of taking away
Everything I've ever loved
It makes the ships sail
When I'm at the shore
Crashes heavy waves
I can only watch
With blurry gaze
Running after broken kites
A broken thread remains
Searching for where it belonged
Wishing for a trace
I can only watch
As it fades away
A dancing drop of fire
Draws me on the wall
The silent killer passes by
I can only watch
Every sight hideaway
The wind has a way
Of taking away
Everything I've ever loved

A dead flower is still beautiful
If left alone
It still embodies its delicate figures
If left untouched
It might even scent from somewhere within
If not breathed
But if you get close
You'll see it's bleak and rusted
But if you touch,
It will turn to ashes
Then merge with nothingness
But if you inhale
You'll breathe in its death
Then it will have nothing left
And maybe just like a dead flower
Some live on

I was at a dead end
And I couldn't tell
How angels were guiding me to hell
I peeked and saw lonely devils in heaven
Indifference and to feel foreign
They said is the worst forfeit
Doesn't matter if you have wings to fly
When they've taken your sky
Doesn't matter if you're in a garden
When you see it as black and white
Doesn't matter if rivers prevail
When fire runs in your veins
Doesn't matter how beauty surrounds you
When the only eyesore left is you
Doesn't matter if paradise is yours
When hell is your home
Doesn't matter if you're alive
When you can no longer die
The angels laughed
But that devil cried
And I left happily
To live familiarity

In my unique tragedies

Tonight the voice doesn't end
It's singing strange descants
Curtains in tune with the wind beside my bed
These words whispered in my head
If it's a song
Then I shall be the words no one ever said
If it's poetry
I shall be the verse no one could ever get
If it's a play
I shall be the stage ominously left
If it's a ballad
I shall be the hasty reciter, running away in a fret
If it's a page
I shall be crumpled, scrawled and partly wet
If it's a rhyme
I shall be the fifteen lined sonnet
And if it's a book
 I shall be the empty space after
The end...

These days sunlight is just another bother
Another annoyance
It belongs to other times
When time used to mean a thing
Warmth was felt
Not another factor
To remind the numb
I'm awake
On a dead morning
I'm here
With a part that is lost
I'm gleaming
Under icy rays
These nights are rendered to lifetimes
Looking up through the window
The moon isn't there
The stars aren't there
Void, black and vacant
The murky sky is a familiar skin
Wrapped all around the dead city
It keeps whirling and twirling
I keep running in the distinct directions
I'm stagnant
In a spinning world
I'm breathless
Beneath an open sky
I'm dreamless
With a wistful heart

The cactus isn't lonely in the desert
It feels belonged, not a hazard
Wearing its prickles like a crown
Unbothered, unknown to the crowd
Never gets hurt, nor is it weak
For what it is, it lets you see
It's the rose those hands carrying
Wrapped in hued plastics
What is it?
Feeble petals, is that it?
Why did it grow?
Apart, alone
Its existence a mistake
It'll take it to its grave
Died for its beauty
But, that was its duty
Conceal its ugliness
A staining secret
No one should know
A pretty rose
Mustn't have thorns

The innocence of you
Can turn into something
The demon's fear...

What if...?
Every word spoken vanished
Every dream was forgotten
No importance weighing you down
No passion burning you within, nothingness
There won't be any more evidence for your heart breaks
Thoughtless mind
There won't be nightmares, dreamless nights
Blank and numb but, at least
There won't be any sorrows to live by

You're a soldier
With no badges
Wear your scattered heart
Proudly in your chest
You're a martyr
With a soul
Let it live
Let it grow old
You're a warrior
With damaged hands
Still catching bullets
Whenever you can
You're a wounded
Who doesn't bleed
But the aching sting
Runs very deep
You're a soldier
In a forgotten battlefield

She can't be cotton
When being woven into steel
The only way to heal
She can't be a rose
With growing thorns
And dying petals
She can't be soft
She can't be fresh
She can't be
Anymore

Shaking hands can't be kissed
Let them be
Hidden
Folded, cautious, helpless
Broken hearts can't be fixed
Let them beat
Unbidden
Coward, sick, needless
Troubled eyes can't be skimmed
Let them see
Within
Averting, appalled, restless
Evaders can't be missed
Let them leave
Ridden
Weary, lost, reckless

The world keeps going
Don't know where but, it keeps going
Being, existing and breathing still
Sometimes I lose my sense of touch
Like you, I've got a million words left to be told
Inside me, they keep on growing
I have a tongue, but ears don't want to hear of such
Hearts would rather be left unknowing
Like you, I want to live again, but sadly I'm already alive
Between clichéd dreams and sweet lies, I'm coping
You've got a free soul, and they call you dead
It's a free world they say but trust me,
we're the ones who are stuck
To all those who left
I'm afraid you're not missing out on so much

Let this fairy tale be done
Before it even begun
Let my heart be yours
I'm better off with none
I'm too old now to believe there is
"The one"
Now I know how life works
No one ever won

Wish there was a way to tell
But how
From where one must begin
When to end
It's long, long chapters
Of nothing but anguishing disasters
And your sympathy will run out
You will tire
The book has a rule
It sounds like a fluke
But the truth is
It's terrified
Not for being plagiarized
But, being used against itself
Every word
Shys away
The book is cursed
Don't read
It'll only hurt

Don't replicate
Bound to hesitate
No word will be spoken
We'll drown in ink I've stolen
To make use of emotion
But you'll drown in vain
And I'm numb to pain
Don't replicate
Stay, don't chase
You can't run away
To the world I've built
Deep in the opaque wilderness
You won't see in that dark
And there's no light in my heart
Don't replicate
The world will get sadder
Everything except you will matter
Cause you'll want it that way
A soul crusher so they don't care
You'll perish but breathe
Don't replicate me

When things no longer matter,
does being hopeful scare you?

To understand the quiet
To learn the silence, ponder about the words
All the words
To understand the detached
Numbness that they have, break your heart and then feel
All at once
To understand a loner, get in a crowd, smile to fit in
Shrink into nothingness
All alone

Are things really that deep?
Or is it merely I who want them to be?
Longing to dive into drops, but end up in its ocean
Is there something hiding behind those flowing curtains?
Or is it merely I who's trying too hard to see?
Searching for stability in the wild winds
And prance to its motion

Leave love when it left you wrecked,
you can't fight destiny...

Running forever just to come last
Maybe that's what happens when
you're running motionless
And when the marathon starts
You've never stopped to begin
But there's a sanctuary in this hopelessness
You've preferred wrecking your own bones
Yet salvage from foreign brokenness
                              Endlessly running just to come last
                                        But you've chosen it

What if hope is a bad thing?
What if it's like a smile, rooting from a smirk
The villain disguised as a hero
Hope ignites an odd fear
What if it will end instead of aiding you?
What if that hope just came to be a happy ending
Of something you wanted to continue
To carry on
To live by
What if that hope will only stay a hope?
And you will just keep on aspiring
Since you're too blinded to see, there is no way
What if hope is a bad thing?

I'm angry with you, don't talk to me, life
We can't seem to understand one another
A second I was happy
You always make me pay the price
 And that is to suffer
You get a meaning with my existence or so I thought
 Now I know we're merely anchored to each other
I waited for you to vary, I believed you might
So you did, but what a bummer

It's like a cycle of rainbows before the storm
Waits till the heart is happy
By sorrow then it tore
Displays roses and lilies
Lets you feel merely the thorns
We are born to dream of heavens
Then why is hell where we go?

Once you know what a human can do...
You'll start to have empathy for Satan

A crash like the waves, however with a slight difference
No one sees
No one hears
Rising simply to hit the ground
Again, and again, and again
Just like the waves, she comes and she goes
Just like the waves, I'm felt deeply
Just like the waves, she's scrawling in the blues
Trying to be ivory and blank
Just like the waves, she comes off strong
But there's a feebleness to it she doesn't want you to see
So she vanished
Just like a random wave that no one witnessed...

I can't stand what's inside me
A soul making connections
With the ones who can never find me
A heart suffers from aggression
Send to it by me
For I'm tired of its attachments
To hell they always guide me

The scariest demons won't even make you move
When you have the scariest life

Mirror breaks
So does my heart
Life came to haunt me again
My feelings change
So does the colour of my face
My life has come to haunt me again
I listen to strange melodies
Merged with the words of strangers
Strangely it calms me down
For my life has come to haunt me again

Hell is
A heart made of glass
In a world made of stones

The poison running down
Through the windows
Of a wounded soul
Burns the peeling skin
It only hurts more

I'm near a pond, about to get drowned
and I'm letting it happen
Will they ever know I'm the one to blame,
or their theories will save my reputation once gone?
I'm near a string attached to my shoulders,
it's strangling me and I'm letting it
Will they ever know
I've been parading to my dead end, all along?
I'm near a pessimist,
it's getting under my skin and I'm letting it
Will they ever know I started it first and ended up l
aughing at our misfortunes doing us wrong?
I'm near a wishing well about to fall
and I'm letting it happen
Will they ever know I wished to hear broken longings,
to know I'm not alone?
I'm near a madman, he's driving me crazy
mumbling of dangers and I'm letting it
Will they ever know how much wiser I got,
while singing for the apocalypse with that stranger?
I'm near an idle flower, it's dying and I'm letting it
Will they ever know it was bypassed for not being a rose,
and it asked me to let it go...

قفس سقف ندارد

مگر تو که بال نداری

صیاد حرف زرار ندارد

مگر تو که خیال نداری

جواب است او کاری ندارد

مگر تو که سوال نداری

پنجره ها ثبات ندارد

مگر تو که اقبال نداری

پایه های پایدار ندارد

مگر تو که روال نداری

شاخه فاصله چندان ندارد

مگر تو که وصال نداری

گذشته دوام ندارد

مگر تو که حال نداری

قفس تو سقف ندارد

مگر تو که بال نداری

Stellar

Perhaps the stardust within us recalls
That darkness is the natural state of the cosmos
To where once it belonged
And now we yearn in the dusk
In search of home

At nights, I'm not me
She's the one who came a long way
She's so strong, yet so weak
Will give the best advice
 Will tell you to believe
She does it herself
But the result is what she can't see
She's the symbol of unrequited
 A fool you have never seen
The one dying for her love is herself indeed
But she's too busy since for others she surely feels
At nights, I'm so me

The pillows hide
They don't want to hear
The screams that are cried
While holding them near
They are scared
Tired of soaking tears

Nightfall
You now seem brighter than my sunny days
Life
How shall I suffer, in what other ways?
Heart
Learn to beat at a calm pace
I infer you're delicate, but don't you dare break
Eyes
Swallow tears, swallow my pains
Tongue
No more ranting honestly, no one cares
Soul
You just carry on in your dying days

I can't be sleepless
Too lethargic to admit
Too afraid to dream
A vision that never ends
Notions I never said
A dreamscape, a stranger
Moments I never met
Either way, it stings
Sheer scenarios
I can't forget

I will count all the stars
But I will never count on you
For you said you wouldn't let me fall
And you were the one to push me, too

I'm deceiving by blinding them luminous
I let my scars shine too, but only I
know how it felt to get them
They see it as inspirations, but sometimes
those scars are all I can see, all that I am
I'm overqualified, so unique
and I want your world to know about it

It's always when I'm shining the brightest
when I hate my light the most
It's always when I'm gazed at when I feel worthless
It's not standing out, it's hanging alone amidst nothingness
And I can't tell to whom I belong
To you who I'm chasing
Or these vacant spaces

Your world flashes before me
And I'm following it
The more I follow, the more our distance cultivates and
I'm afraid, I'm finding comfort in the void between
I don't get close enough to anything,
nor can anything get close enough to me
I've gotten addicted to empty spaces,
I wrap it all around me, and I feel it to my core

It's so quiet in here, but sometimes...I like the way
the wind softly whistles, the way cars pass
and that little girl looks at me from the window seat

Dear earth, you're nothing but a song made
up of sad lyrics, but happy melodies and these
humans of yours never learned how to sing it.
They gaze at me and enjoy my silence in tranquillity

I'm an unbothered piece of decoration,
dangling above apocalypses
Your helplessness kills me, and my incapability
is my nightmare, then I go into hiding

Unhurriedly fading away is the way
I say my hasty goodbyes
By acting shallow, I can drown in myself peacefully
But, I'll be back, you don't have another
Luna, and I don't have another earth
We're bound to each other's tragedies,
and with them, we fell in love...

موده شدی در انتظار، حق نشنیدیم

ی خاموشی تو را می سرایم

، لبت رماد شد و ما فقط دیدیم

را با خون شهیدانت می آرایم

وس دیروزت چادر سفید پوش شد

که بر سر و مظلومانه میخندد دلربایم

ـ بر آن کودک که پدر رفت و او مرد شد

دستان کوچک و محکوک او را می ستایم

. ما قربان نمی خواهد مدتیست

ـ سر ملهوف میشوند فدایم

نم زیستانیم، مشتاق قیامت

سمان تیر آلود تو راه نیابد ندایم

ن بیگانگی مکن

ن جای آرامی برایم

Coda

Collect your broken pieces
Be proud
You loved in a world
That is constantly watered
By pure hate

There's a bloom
In that rusting room
Please don't touch
Stay far enough
Please don't pity
Petals falling bitty
You don't know
Let it grow, there alone
It might be dark
It might be forlorn, but the moonlight falls
When you close the door
And expectedly go
The rust glimmers
As the blossom shimmers
Under the spotlight, on nights
It's not depressive, but a festive
Of melancholic, brokenhearted
Sauntering torn diamonds
To the golden silence
At last

Despite it all
No one ever sang a song
That would be so sad
The perfect amount of sadness
Generous like the bestower of dismay
Sometimes it takes more sorrow
To stop that spreading hollow
And sometimes that's what happens
To arid eyes
So let me be fey
And let me sing
And let me sway
Burning wings
To my dying days
I want a song to sing
Despite it all
No one ever found
A way to kill the pain
With something other than pain
Sometimes it takes a force
Stronger than what wrecked
To amend
And sometimes that's what happens
To broken heart
So let me be fey
And let me sing
And let me sway
Burning wings
To douse my ablaze
I want a song to sing
For my dying days
I want a song to sing

I'm broken
My cracks are beautiful
They are art
The artist is life

Can I for once?
Do what they don't
Run on the streets
Not on the pathways
Dream in days, under the sunlight
Sing and dance under the moonlight
Scream as obnoxiously as I can
Not swallow my emotions
Cry rivers and oceans
Laugh louder at my mistakes
Embrace my clumsiness
Forgive my soul
Live life as I want to
Not the way it should be

But this pain
It makes artists bleed
Thick blood
That eats them up
They call it paint
On the portrait
And they just see
As he bleeds
Secretly
But this pain
It makes writers speak
Who don't have a voice
Who've built homes in the void
Who didn't have a choice
But to disappear
Internally
But this pain
Will make a sage out of you
But this pain
Won't let you break a heart
But this pain
Assassinates
Beautifully

You're not alone
Look around
You will see somehow
There are tiny fairies
In the midst of a passing breeze
You're not alone
There's her touch, her fain
Amid pouring rain
You're not alone
In your heartbeats, a million souls rest
The ones you haven't even met yet
You're not alone
She speaks to you
Through those symphonies and muse
You're not alone
An amber, spherical smile
Gleams above you all night
Whoever smiled rear
Shall never be alone, nor fear
You're looked after
Despite all your disasters
When anguish embarks to grow
Know that you're never alone

If I could
I would paint a frame for you to remember me
Hues of rainbows
Blue will be stolen from the oceans
Like the depth of what we had
A touch of brown mountains to show we stood tall
We had it strong
The frame slowly turns into a picture
We never captured
Don't miss, I was never caught
Only remember if you must
When I'll be gone

The baby blue sky
Near the palm trees
Across the seas
A wind passes by
Closes my eyes
Nourishes within
A cold breeze holds me
Takes away the memories
Fades away, slowly like sunlight

I never knew
I deserved happiness
Until I earned it
By pure devastation

I look at the sky
Leave a message for you
And imagine...
You'll hear

I want to heal like the fragile flowers
And bloom as if it's spring
I want to sing like the free birds
As if I had their wings
I want to rise like the sun
As if I've never been torn down
I want to flow like the rivers
Drown in them my sins
I want to stand strong like the mountains
As if I was born like that
I want to turn into a star
By accepting my failures
I want to win

Just a deep breath
A sweet moment to be reminded
And you'll be able
To move on...

I got lost somewhere
Somewhere with a dusty air
Elevated willows
Smoky clouds
A path to nowhere
Changes to colours, I err to describe
Now rainbows appear peaky in here
A land with fairies
A sky full of stars
I feel real in this fantasy
Please don't take me far
I got lost somewhere
I found me
I got stuck somewhere
I feel free

At least...
We gaze at the same moon
Live under the same sky
And share the same light of the sun

Never let those scars forbid you from shining
—The moon

I hope you answer for yourself the
questions you're dying to be asked...

And at the end
There is nothing
But the memories
Which left us wheezing
Till we teared up
Yet, now we tear up silently
Remembering them...

Samman Akbarzada

I do not need to tell you anything about me because you will already know too much after reading these pages—and that haunts me. But by being vulnerable, I know we can make other people brave.

I am an Afghan woman in my early twenties. Today I am a refugee in a beautiful but very foreign country. The story of why I am here begins, literally, with a story. I was inspired to write my debut novel, Life is a Movie, by the kid I used to see selling cotton candy near my school. It is the story of a working child trying to save his perishing mother in Kabul, Afghanistan. In my book, I recount the crises that women face in our society on a daily basis and what life is like for them—what it feels like under the unbearable consequences of war and the Taliban.

We cannot empower women until we highlight the oppressions they are forced to withstand. In Afghanistan, there are many girls left behind, some I used to know and continue to hold out hope for. But, I no longer know what to tell them, so I dedicate this book to them and all Afghan women, wherever they might be.

We did not deserve this. The angst of how voiceless Afghans have become is demoralizing, but I will never keep quiet nor watch my country perish silently. This is what inspires me to write.

I am too young to be writing about widows, working children, blood, and war. But I guess I never got the chance to experience a life that the world might consider normal. Maybe one day, I will write happier poems, happier stories.

For now, however, I can only make people sad with the laments that my motherland expects me to inscribe for its never-ending funeral.

My book was globally available on the 22nd of August, 2021. I stared at the ceiling that night, wondering what might happen if they, the Taliban, found out about it. The first line of the book's blurb reads "Her husband is killed by the Taliban," and there I was, watching them from behind draped windows as they clenched their Kalashnikovs (automatic rifles) while patrolling streets. I hope you never get to experience how that feels!

No human being should have to experience what it is like to see their motherland crumbling before their eyes. Throughout my life, I have gone through some extremely difficult times. Still, the recent catastrophe in Afghanistan was my first experience feeling like I could not see a future for myself, a future where I am seen as a free soul, respected as a human being, supported to chase my dreams, and given the strength to live strong.

I hope you never have to endure what it feels like to have to erase your name and take refuge from your existence because it could be life-threatening. No name, no dreams, no identity, no sense of self; I went everywhere and deleted traces of my existence and whatever I had achieved so far. I had been so looking forward to the day my book would be published. I thought it would be the happiest day of my life, but instead, I wound up dreading it like an upcoming funeral. I was terrified for myself and my family.

I wanted to do more and continue with my writing journey. However, I could not utilize my skills there anymore. And it was too dangerous a place for us to live. Therefore, my family and I had to flee. Even with an abundance of help from people who made me realize that God does send angels to rescue us, still, our journey was filled with suffocating nights that I thought would never end. Nevertheless, we managed to escape.

Sometimes this uncertain thought enters my head—am I happy to lose my country and live as an outsider all my life? And that thought frightens me. Then I see those who are helping me, and I feel hopeful for a bright and successful future. My dear family and my sweetest friends, without them, I am nothing. I would also like to take this opportunity to thank some of the angels responsible for my rescue—Mrs. Allyson, Mr. John, Mrs. Cathy, and Mr. Orin. You have been a dream team. Kindness does not feel foreign anymore; you recovered my hope in humanity.

For Afghans, life has been an everlasting terror. We have been in pain forever. But no matter what, I will try my best to get through it because I know this is not the end, chapters are awaiting us, and the young people of Afghanistan are our best and only hope. One day, Afghanistan will be free from oppression. Even after all that has happened, I have faith and believe this with my entire heart and soul.

Through writing, I want to play my little part. I want to paint a picture of what I think the world should look like; how it should accept its collective responsibility to build nations where children are not victims of greedy warlords, where women do not have to fight to be seen as human beings, and where peace is real, tangible, and even palpable— not merely a wish on a shooting star. I will always strive to use whatever talents and abilities I have to do whatever I can, as best I can, for all my fellow citizens held hostage and suffering behind closed doors because I have so much love and hope for them.

I derive my sense of self from what soothes me the most, gives me sustenance, befriends me, completes me, and, ultimately, gives greater meaning to my life; I am talking about writing, my identity. Through writing, I found a voice and the solace I had never experienced before discovering this wondrous passion. Writing has helped save my life, literally. It has helped me escape war, possibly even death, so writing was, is, and always will be life-changing for me.

I have been passionate about writing since a young age. My first inspiration came when I used to watch my mother waking up late at night with a pen to portray her love and sorrow for her country in poetry, and that shaped me; whatever I am, whatever success I may acquire, it is all because of her. The first ten Dari poems you will find in these pages are written by her, and I am glad to have the honor of sharing them with you. The Queen writes under the pen name Jina Khamosh.

At first, my writings were all rainbows and sunshine, but as I got older and tasted a bit of life, I noticed that it has a much larger purpose than merely my own pleasure. Sure, writing is my respite, but time transformed it into the weapon I wield as a voice for the silenced. My habitual trope has turned into something for which I find myself running out of sad words; narrating the same sad stories is sometimes wearying. The sci-fi characters, sweet fantasy, kings and queens, dragons and witches are locked away from me, and I struggle to catch a glimpse of them. All I see are malnourished children, sad eyes of women, one-legged men, and the God-forsaken realm. The world has become numb to my country's pain. I do not want to; may I never stop hurting.

I had never imagined that this was what writing would become for me. Sometimes I want to set aside the laptop, tear up the papers, and never have to think about ways to make life miserable for the doomed people that I make up. But then what? I end up thinking about the real versions of them.

I have included a lot of what I have seen, heard, and experienced in my works as if I have left fragments of myself in parts of it. There is not a day that goes by without me holding my pen, sitting, and portraying my deepest thoughts on a piece of paper as if I am giving life to it and a will to myself.

Here, my sole purpose is to let you taste my versions of melancholy and, through the same pessimistic lenses, let you discern that survival is possible, even for you and even for me. I hope that sharing my fragments will make it easier for all of us.

When I left Kabul, our land might have been burning, but the sky was blue. And the epiphany struck me that they could not ruin Afghanistan's sky. When there is a way for the light to come in, there will come a day when the darkness will end—it is inevitable. Here's to that day.

instagram.com/sammanwrites
sammanakbarzada@gmail.com

THOUGHT CATALOG Books

Thought Catalog Books is a publishing imprint of Thought Catalog, a digital magazine for thoughtful storytelling, and is owned and operated by The Thought & Expression Company, an independent media group based in the United States of America. Founded in 2010, we are committed to helping people become better communicators and listeners to engender a more exciting, attentive, and imaginative world. The Thought Catalog Books imprint connects Thought Catalog's digital-native roots with our love of traditional book publishing. The books we publish are designed as beloved art pieces. We publish work we love. Pioneering an author-first and holistic approach to book publishing, Thought Catalog Books has created numerous best-selling print books, audiobooks, and eBooks that are being translated in over 30 languages.

ThoughtCatalog.com | **Thoughtful Storytelling**

ShopCatalog.com | **Shop Books + Curated Products**